SAVING YOUR RAINFOREST MIND

A Guided Journal

for the Curious, Creative,
Smart, & Sensitive

PAULA PROBER

LUMINARE PRESS
WWW.LUMINAREPRESS.COM

SAVING YOUR RAINFOREST MIND
A Guided Journal for the Curious, Creative, Smart, & Sensitive
Copyright © 2023 by Paula Prober

Printed in the United States of America

Design by Claire Flint Last

Luminare Press
442 Charnelton St.
Eugene, OR 97401
www.luminarepress.com

LCCN: 2023907105
ISBN: 979-8-88679-273-7

"Inner work helps you untangle life's intricate, sticky vines and gain clarity about what real love might look like, feel like, and be. It allows you to break old family cycles and legacies and find new nourishing, nurturing pathways. Pathways to love. Pathways to higher love, generous love, divine love."

Contents

Introduction

"

All people who have rainforest minds
are gifted but not all gifted folks
have rainforest minds.

How to Use This Guided Journal

- Do you worry often about the meaning of life, the future of the planet, the nature of reality, and how to contribute to creating a peaceful world?

- Do your many sensitivities often run amok?

- Do people tell you to lower your standards when you wish they would raise theirs?

- Were you accused of being a know-it-all in school when you were really a want-to-know-it-all?

- Is your big, soft, lonely heart breaking on a regular basis?

These are some of the many questions you will be exploring as you dive into this guided journal. Before you begin, there are a few important things I want to share with you, so please read on.

If you know me, you know I use an analogy to describe folks like you. If you don't know me, you will soon! You have what I call a rainforest mind (RFM). Like the rainforest, you're highly sensitive, creative, resourceful, resilient, intense, and smart, yet you're often misunderstood. Other traits and experiences may include perfectionism, intuition, very high standards and expectations, multi-potentiality, loving learning but frustration with schooling, extraordinary empathy, loneliness, anxiety, existential depression, difficulty with decisions, and a deep desire to create a better world for all. You might recognize these traits as belonging to people we call gifted. I use that term occasionally here, because rainforest-minded people are gifted. If you don't identify with that word, no problem. Keep reading anyway.

I have a background in working with gifted children in public schools and then counseling and consulting with gifted adults. Because definitions of giftedness are varied and controversial, I find the rainforest analogy a simpler and more accurate descriptor, so don't fret about the gifted label. You belong here if you're curious, creative, smart, and sensitive, or as one of my blog readers put it, "twisty turn-y, deep thought-y, and mystical realm-y."

There are many journal writing books and websites available these days, yet they may not include some of your particular rainforest-y issues. This journal is designed specifically for you, and it includes relevant topics such as sensitivities, hiding your intelligence, existential depression, intuitive abilities, rejection and misunderstanding, relationships, decisions and multipotentiality, anxiety, schooling, complexity, and more.

This guided journal is your opportunity to take a deep dive into the highly sensitive seeker that is you. You'll be shown how to increase your understanding, acceptance, and celebration of your multiple complexities through writing prompts, questions, structured exercises, and examples from my own journals. You'll create, analyze, draw, design, visualize, laugh, and cry as you take the journey to find your authentic voice and paths to your uniquely passionate, powerful, and purposeful life.

I'll be your guide as you grapple with your fears, doubts, questions, conundrums, and mysteries. I'll be here as you untangle the sticky vines and explore, examine, and revive the exuberant life force that is you. I'll be your guide to recovering your strength, authenticity, and magnificence. The magnificence that may have been crushed under the pressure to be smartest, under the bully's taunts, the schooling frustrations, the expectations of exemplary achievement and traditional success, the devastating loneliness, the racism, homophobia, or antisemitism, the overwhelm, the underwhelm, or the rubble of your ancestral baggage. I've included my own journal entries in a section at the end of the book so you know I've done my own grappling, a good amount of climbing out of the dysfunctional family legacy, and recovering and celebrating my authenticity and radiance.

You don't need to work through this book from front to back. Find the pages you're drawn to and start there. Your nonlinear, intuitive mind will take you where you need to go. Each page has an explanation and suggested ideas. I want you to have a rich, varied experience but, at the same time, don't want to overwhelm you. Pick the exercises that appeal to you and skip others. You may come back to them later or ignore them forever. There's a lot here, so take your time.

I have provided space to write and draw, but it may not be enough for your deepest dives and certainly not for your complex art projects or intricate mind maps! You may want your own blank book or laptop to fully address some of the prompts and suggestions. Keep your art supplies handy, too.

If you're unfamiliar with the RFM concept, it might be helpful to read the entire book before starting the exercises. There is also my first book, *Your Rainforest Mind: A Guide to the Well-Being of Gifted Adults and Youth*. It provides in-depth descriptions of the important issues via case studies of my counseling and consulting clients.

This is not a substitute for good therapy, in case you were wondering. If you've experienced trauma, ideally, you'll find a therapist, too. If some of these exercises trigger a lot of anxiety, that's another clue you might need to find a counselor, but for now, let me be your guide. I shall walk with you. I know the landscape well, being a journaling-maniac rainforest-minder myself.

I was going to title this book *Managing the Mosquitoes in Your Rainforest Mind* but was afraid it might turn up in online searches for insect repellant! The thought about the mosquitoes came from this comment on LinkedIn from Philippe in Paris:

> I remember one of your quotes where you said something like "I'm here to remind you that your rainforest mind is a thing of beauty. Even with all those mosquitoes." I believe I finally reached a point where I'm fine with my brain and all the fractals inside but for god's sake how do we manage the mosquitoes!?

This book is about guiding you to get fine with your brain-mind-body-heart-soul-spirit and all its fractals while helping you manage the mosquitoes and maybe, in the process, create a more peaceful world.

So from our twisty turn-y, deep thought-y, mystical realm-y selves, let us dive in.

The Quick and Easy Guide to Rainforest-Mindedness

1. Do your many sensitivities often run amok?

2. Are you flummoxed by your multitudes?

3. Do people tell you to lower your standards when you wish they would raise theirs?

4. Do you wonder how people miss what is so obvious to you?

5. Do you worry regularly that you're not as smart as everyone says you are and/or hide your intelligence under the sofa with the dust mites?

6. Do you worry about the meaning of life, the future of the planet, the nature of reality, and how to contribute to creating a peaceful world?

7. Do you worry incessantly about your worrying?

8. Do you find simple things to be difficult and complex things easy?

9. Have you found it impossible to find someone who wants to dive as deeply into the nuances of (fill in the blank with your favorite books) as you do?

10. Do people tell you to stop overthinking when you wish they would stop underthinking?

11. Are you soothed by your conversations with trees, rivers, and birds?

12. Are you spooked by the accuracy of your premonitions?

13. Are you searching for the person who can keep up with you, maybe even surpass you?

14. Is your big, soft, lonely heart breaking on a regular basis?

15. Were you accused of being a know-it-all in school when you were really a want-to-know-it-all?

16. Do you wince when the word *gifted* is applied to you because you know how much you don't know, you know people who are smarter, and you care deeply about equity and justice?

If you answered yes to more than half of these and ruminated about the rest, chances are good that you have a rainforest mind.

> Journaling is a private, vulnerable experience. I've come to think of the journal as a sacred container, where you show up as your most unedited self. Each journal entry is a glimpse of what you think and feel at a given time on a given day, and we often admit things we wouldn't say out loud...
>
> —Suleika Jaouad, *The Isolation Journals*

Exploring
Your Layers

"

You may feel like a weirdo because no one you know adores gathering new words, understands string theory, or groks the many layers of your intricate mind palace.

Therapy Is Now Popular

I t appears that therapy is now popular. Some therapists on Instagram have thousands of followers. You're no longer a weirdo if you talk about your therapist. That's a relief! As you might imagine, I'm a strong advocate for counseling. It has made a big difference in my life— all the difference, really. In an article in the August 1, 2022 issue of *The New York Times*, Alyson Krueger wrote about how more folks on dating apps are looking for someone who has been in therapy, so now you can be part of a movement!

Being a therapist for many years, I've seen how it soothes, heals, strengthens, and transforms, but I know it can be hard to find a therapist who can keep up. Someone who isn't overwhelmed by your intelligence and intensity. Someone who can see through your capacity to articulate your pain and mask your depression, can see through to your despair, utter loneliness, and serious trauma. With a good therapist, you're joined on your journey into the dark night of your soul that should not be faced alone.

Even though I worked with different therapists over the years as a client and with healing arts such as energy work, acupuncture, breath work, massage, and astrology, I always had my journal for processing, expressing, and analyzing what happened in the sessions. It was also useful for the times when I needed a friend, when therapy was not available, or when I was taking a break from counseling. Reading journal entries to my therapist was powerful, too. Being witnessed. Being heard. Being held in a safe, trustworthy embrace. Whether or not you have a therapist now, your journal is your guide, counselor, and trusted friend.

Write a letter to your journal. Give your journal a name, if you like. What are your hopes, expectations, needs, and desires? Tell your journal some of your secrets. Feel your connection as you imagine this journal as your friend and as you embark on this sacred journey together. Draw. Doodle.

Imagine a younger part of you who is lonely and wanting to meet you. Write a description of the child part. Imagine the child in a beautiful, protected, cozy place. Give the child art supplies, books, a pet, and/or whatever they need. Consider building a relationship with this younger part, and write letters or a conversation where you begin to connect. If this is difficult, come back to it later, but leave the child with a loving team of guides, angels, or witches. If you have an old photo, include it here. Build a small altar to the child with photos and objects they would love. If working with child parts sounds appealing but overwhelming, get *No Bad Parts* by Richard Schwartz and follow his directions to understand your many aspects including your Higher Self. Internal Family Systems (IFS) therapy is a great structure to follow on your own or with a counselor. You might need a separate journal just for that.

Take a moment to get quiet and tune in to your body. Imagine there is a place where an inner advisor, a Higher Self, or your intuition lives. Where do you feel this? Take your time. Trust what you feel. Breathe into it, and build a deeper connection through writing, art, and/or visualization. Start a conversation. Give yourself time to trust that you will hear your wisdom.

Do Your Many Sensitivities
Often Run Amok?

C hances are you already identify as a highly sensitive person and have read books or listened to podcasts about this. Even so, you may wonder what you can do to manage, accept, and appreciate what may feel overwhelming and uncomfortable at times.

Make a list of your specific sensitivities: smells, tastes, colors, textures, noises, chemicals, emotions, medications, leaf blowers, violent movies, the suffering of others, intuitions, plants speaking to you, synchronicities, spiritual guides, and more. Let it be as long as it needs to be. Often these sensitivities are considered liabilities. Reread your list. Which ones are actually strengths? Put stars next to the strengths.

Get creative and imagine how your sensitivities serve you. Are you a better healer, musician, artist, or parent because of them? Perhaps your plants thrive because you talk to them. You're kinder and gentler. You save money by not going to violent movies or needing large amounts of medication. You can diagnose illnesses by their smells and tastes, which makes you a popular practitioner. You're a great friend. What else?

Write about the sensitivities you find difficult. Do loud noises make you irritable? Do you have to paint your living room twelve times to get it right? Are these modifiable in any way, or how might you set boundaries to reduce your exposure? For the sensitivities you have some control over, make a plan to adjust, adapt, ignore, or transform. For the sensitivities you cannot change in some way, make peace with them. Write this: *I make peace with my…I accept I am highly sensitive. It may be frustrating, but I'm okay.* How might you be kind to yourself?

Make a collage or drawing that illustrates your life when overwhelmed, and then make another that feels like peace, calm, and quiet.

"

Let curiosity be your extreme sport.

Do People Tell You to Lower Your Standards When You Wish They Would Raise Theirs?

t's likely that you have high standards and expectations for your work, your relationships, and your life. The word "perfectionist" is often used to describe this way of being. I've seen two types of perfectionism in RFMs. In the healthy (intrinsic) version, you're driven to create beauty, balance, harmony, justice, and precision. Are you obsessed with finding just the right words? The exact shade of yellow? A perfect melody? A gorgeous sunset? A detailed, nuanced, meticulous presentation of the scientific concept you're researching? Do you feel a deep satisfaction, sometimes even joy, when you find it? It's interesting how we admire Olympic athletes as they strive for this type of achievement but see it as weakness or elitism when it's in intellectual realms.

Can you give yourself permission to maintain your highest standards without expecting others to have them too? Can you find ways to prioritize your projects so you maintain your standards when it really matters but loosen them, on occasion, when it doesn't matter so much? (For example, when writing an email to your Aunt Mildred.)

Write about what striving for perfection looks like for you. When are you in the midst of a healthy perfectionism adventure? Describe it. What if you loved this about yourself? What if you saw it as a strength, even as a way to make a contribution to the betterment of humankind?

Design a mantra to remind yourself that you have a right to your perfectly persnickety ways, perhaps something like *I'm driven to create at the highest level possible and feel the joy it brings even if no one else understands.* Write/design your mantra on a card, and place it where you will see it every day. Make a little art project from it. Build an altar to your excellence.

Can you differentiate between this healthy drive and the unhealthy version where you're terrified of failure? Where making a small mistake feels like the end of the world? I call this extrinsic or unhealthy perfectionism.

Make two lists. In one, write more examples of how you experience pleasure through striving for the precise note, color, word, conversation, dance experience, technological advancement, or recipe. Describe the feeling of satisfaction, pleasure, or even joy when this type of perfection is achieved. For me, I compare it to those fleeting moments dancing the Argentine tango when both dancers are so utterly connected that they are one heart and four legs. Perfection. Joy. I also feel deep satisfaction when I complete a blog post that has the tone, language, and message that fit together in a smooth, tight, a-little-funny package. On the other list, write examples of times when you were paralyzed by a need to be the best or smartest or to prove to someone how much you knew.

One way to manage unhealthy perfectionism is to work with your critical voice. Start a dialogue. Ask it why it is so noisy, so determined. What is it trying to protect you from? Is there a way it might step back and let you make mistakes without berating you? Is your critical voice a parental figure? A teacher? What does it need from you in order to agree to calm down? You may need to have many conversations. Over time, you may become friends, or at least it will loosen its hold over you. Imagine that you can strive for wholeness or balance instead of perfection.

Perhaps you feel pressure to be a high achiever because you've been told how smart you are since you were little; this has become your identity or what you believe makes you lovable. What would you like to say to your child self about that now? What makes that little one lovable? Compassion? Kindness? Curiosity? Drive? Sense of humor? Write them a love letter, pointing out their strengths. See if they want to write back to you or just curl up in your lap.

When Failure Is Failure and
When It Is Not

wonder if you have a particularly challenging relationship to failure. Many RFMs do because of the pressure they feel to be a high achiever because they are "so smart," as mentioned earlier.

Make a list of your so-called failures. Analyze it carefully. How many are insignificant now that time has passed and you're less connected to them? How many took you to new adventures that you would not have had otherwise? How many are mistakes but not really failures? How many are losses but not failures? How many might you use to make your memoir memorable?

Do you see how you're redefining failure? A mistake is not a failure unless it's a huge mistake like taking the wrong baby home from the hospital or driving your car into a tree. Those are big mistakes but not really failures. Right? What about losses? Maybe you lost the game. Did you fail, or did you just lose?

Perhaps the biggest shift to make is to understand that a failure is a thing that happens, but it is not who you are. You might say, "I may have failed at this, but I'm not a failure as a person." It's an important distinction. This could be hard if you grew up being blamed or abused or were the scapegoat in the family. You may have to practice saying that mantra over and over. "I may have failed at…but I'm not a failure as a person."

If this topic is particularly tough, here are ways to make friends with failure. Have conversations with it to get to know it better. Write an "Ode to Failure." Design a comic book honoring your failures and how they taught you something.

In other words, reduce the power of failure in your life. This will be particularly important if you have children. They'll be much more relaxed about making mistakes if you are too. There is a saying that goes something like this: "If you're not failing, you're thinking too small." Go bigger and fail often or at least occasionally. Okay?

"

Just because you're extremely
articulate and can describe your deep,
existential depression and anxiety
in great detail to your therapist
while being successful at your job
doesn't mean you're fine and
don't need therapy.

Metaphorically Speaking—
You Are the Symphony,
They Are the Trombones

You know the metaphor of the rainforest mind. You are the rainforest. Complex. Intense. Creative. Colorful. Sensitive. Misunderstood. Resourceful. Resilient.

What other metaphor or analogy might describe you? Are you like a cathedral to others who are like studio apartments? Are you a Corvette to their Ramblers? What metaphor fits for you? How does it match your complexity? Your sensitivity? You are the sky, they are the stars? You are the whole enchilada, they are the guacamole? You are the symphony, they are the trombones? You are the elaborately customized and restored VW bus, they are the gas-guzzling sports car? Oh, this is fun. You get the idea. Don't worry about sounding conceited or unkind. This is just for you!

Write a detailed description of your metaphor. Draw it. Paint it. Make it 3D. Can you choose a metaphor that allows you to be more connected to others? If the rainforest is still the most fitting, draw your rainforest self, or create a collage from those old *National Geographic* magazines stored in the attic at your grandmother's house.

The Benefits of
"Failed" Partnerships

S peaking of failure, good partnerships can be hard to find, and when they end, it can feel devastating. Loneliness is often an issue for RFMs, because it seems the Universe has not created a whole bunch of us. What can you do when a partnership ends?

Make a list of your "failed" partnerships. (You can include friendships, if you like.) See if you can find what they have in common. How are the partners similar? As you reflect, were there red flags that you ignored? This processing is not easy. Books by Harville Hendrix provide specific guidance along with books by John Welwood and anything by Esther Perel or Alain de Botton.

Just because a relationship ends doesn't mean it's a failure. Maybe it was a good decision to end it. Maybe you both received what you needed and it was time to move on. Perhaps your partner was unwilling to do deep inner work, so the relationship could not evolve. It's also possible that unhealthy patterns were being replayed. Maybe you were afraid of getting too close for fear of abandonment. Perhaps the relationship reminded you or your partner of patterns in your family of origin that you did not want to see. The more you examine what happened, the more clarity you will find, and this will inform future relationships.

We often select partners who reflect unresolved issues from our past. It gives you the opportunity to heal the issues if you and the partner are willing to examine the patterns that come up or if the end of the relationship leads you to therapy!

As an RFM, there might be additional complexities. It is likely you will experience loneliness over the years. Due to your intellectual needs, capacity to learn quickly, and competence in many areas, plus your sensitivities and empathy, it's hard to find others like you for friendship—partnership, even more so. When you find someone, anxiety, self-doubt, and fear of failure may get stirred up, not to mention the family of origin material that we all run into.

Pick a relationship that was particularly difficult. Write about it in the form of a story where you figure out in the end what you were supposed to learn. If you have enough distance from it, see if you can find the humor. You may need to do some therapy before you can get to the education you received or any laughs.

When to Say Yes and
When to Say No

D o you have trouble setting boundaries? Do people often ask for your help and you give it because you can, even if you don't have the time or energy, because you feel you should? Because you have the most skills? Because you feel guilty for being gifted? This is another conundrum for many RFMs. It may be true that you would be able to complete the task more quickly and thoroughly, so you feel an obligation to do it, but if you say yes to everything that you can do more quickly and thoroughly, you'll become undone, unglued, or overwhelmed.

If a particular person who is taking advantage of your generosity comes to mind, write a letter that you don't send, expressing your resentment, anger, or limits. You don't need to be polite, as this person will not be reading it. After writing it, make a list of statements you can say to this person next time they ask for a favor. For example:

"Let me think about it and get back to you."

"I know I have done this for you in the past, but I think this is something you can do yourself. Perhaps you're underestimating your abilities."

"I appreciate your faith in me, but I don't have the time or energy right now for this."

"I'm learning how to set healthy limits, and I feel safe practicing on you. Thanks."

If you find setting boundaries difficult, there might be something more complex going on, possibly originating in your childhood. There may have been expectations, pressures, or rules you were not allowed to break. There may have been abuse, and it was dangerous to say no. If this was the case, it may feel dangerous now even though you are safe. If you find yourself in these situations over and over, you might need the help of a therapist to sort it all out. You may also have difficulty speaking up in situations where there is an unequal balance of power. These situations may be complex and require the support of an ally.

Boundary setting is a complicated adventure, so go easy on yourself. If these exercises create too much anxiety, get a cup of tea and come back to this at another time.

Complete any of the following sentences. It will likely bring insight into what is beneath your difficulty with boundaries.

"I can't say no because…" _____
_____
_____

"If I say no, then…" _____
_____
_____

"I must always say yes because…" _____
_____
_____

"It's dangerous to say no because…" _____
_____
_____

"

Not everyone sees what you see, feels what you feel, or knows what you know. They see black, white, and gray. You see all the colors and the multiple subtle shades within each. It is magnificent, overwhelming, and lonely.

Does Your Empathy Overwhelm You?

A lot is written these days about empathy and empaths. There are online conferences such as from The Shift Network where you can find tools and techniques. You might need help identifying where your empathy starts and ends and where reactivity to old, dysfunctional family patterns begins. You might need help defining the limits of your compassion. Empathy and compassion may come easily to you but overwhelm you emotionally, physically, and spiritually. When and how do you set clear boundaries? (Boundaries, again??) When you have a rainforest mind, you might find people taking advantage of your skills and kindness. How do you learn to say no to unreasonable demands or even reasonable ones? If you're capable of doing what someone asks, it doesn't mean you have to say yes. How do you know when you're interpreting your empathy accurately?

Think of your relationships with friends, relatives, and kids and examples of your interactions and experiences. Jot down memories of times when your empathy was helpful to you or someone else. Then list times when you felt too much or confused someone else's feelings for your own.

Write a list of reminders that help you manage your empathy and recognize when boundaries are needed. Here are some examples:

"It's not unusual for someone with my level of empathy to feel overwhelmed in certain situations even if no one else is aware of it."

"I don't need to provide support or answers to everyone who asks even if I'm the best person for the job."

"I breathe deeply and keep the emotion moving so it doesn't get stuck in my body."

"My emotions may be intense right now because I'm feeling someone else's discomfort. I let go of their discomfort and don't need to rescue them. If my body stays relaxed, the tension I feel will keep moving. I can sway or shake or tap to release the unwanted emotion. I can visualize the tension moving out of my feet into the ground."

"I have a right to leave a situation when the level of emotion/pain/suffering I feel is too high to handle safely."

Consider the idea that in many cases, you can substitute compassion for empathy. In other words, you can care for someone but don't need to deeply feel their pain. You stay separate from their emotions. You care but don't merge with them. This may take a lot of practice as your empathy is likely automatic, but it's worth exploring.

When you have so much empathy, you may have an automatic response to shrink, shut down, or try to disappear when in public and confronted by something uncomfortable. What if it was a safer choice to get bigger, expand, and breathe more deeply? It may seem counterintuitive, but it can help when you feel overwhelmed. Instead of becoming tense and shut down, allow the energy to keep moving. It can move through you and out your feet into the earth. You're bigger than the emotion coming at you. You breathe and expand, and it goes right by you or through you. What image works for you to represent your expansion? Oneness with a tree? A large house with many rooms? Wonder Woman? Batman? Can you draw your expanded self? What colors would you use?

Think of a situation when you felt overwhelmed, and write about it. In your mind's eye, see yourself expanding so that the situation becomes small and unimportant. Write the different outcome where you stay calm and unaffected by the other person or situation. Granted, there will be times when you need to move away from a person, sit near the door, or leave the room. Can you think of times when you needed to set clear boundaries with someone who was too toxic to be around? Make a list of names and situations. Remind yourself that healthy boundaries are important. Everyone benefits when boundaries are set and kept. What image comes to mind that represents good boundaries—light surrounding you? A tiger by your side? A locked door? A guardian angel? Draw or write about it.

Move Your Existential Depression

There could be many reasons for having bouts of existential depression. For one, you are paying attention, and your capacity to seek justice, feel the suffering of others, care about future generations, and be self-critical might contribute to your angst and despair. Because you have a particularly finely tuned nervous system, there might be other factors to consider. You might be sensitive to certain foods and medicines that throw you off balance. Hormones, chemicals, textures, allergies, and illnesses might affect your body-mind so you feel sad or depressed for reasons that are hard to identify. Maybe you feel depressed because you think you haven't lived up to what you feel are your responsibilities or haven't changed the world. Perhaps you're experiencing racism or other forms of discrimination. We live in challenging times.

Write a letter to your depression. See it as a part of you but not all of you, even if it takes up a lot of your energy and time. Imagine it has something to teach you or show you. Picture your depression. What are the colors, shapes, textures? Draw it. If you're so inclined, sing it. Give your depression a song, a voice. Dance it. How does it move? You may think depression doesn't move, but see what happens when you move your depression.

Where do you feel depression in your body? Imagine that it's hiding other feelings. You may feel numb because you're afraid to feel sadness, grief, loss, or despair. Go to that place in your body, and move inside of it. Hold it in your arms. Sing to it. See if breaking through the numbness gives you relief even if you feel more painful emotions.

Write your feelings about the state of the world. Are you overwhelmed? Angry? Frightened? Disappointed? Put your feelings into an art project. You might feel relief by moving more deeply into your emotions. It can open you to creative ideas you might have otherwise missed. It might provide the direction and motivation you need to take action. Share your feelings with a friend or your puppy or kitty.

If you feel depressed because of politics, climate, racism, family, loneliness, illness, or other factors, take a moment and acknowledge that you can only handle these stresses for so long and need to take breaks. Perhaps your numbness is that break. Instead of depression, consider taking a break via denial and compartmentalization. Seriously, there are times when it's okay to put your concerns away.

Consider gathering up your grief and handing it over to the earth, God, your guides, or your Higher Self. Find healthy ways to nourish and refill yourself. Find your community, and reach out. Tune in to a loving field that you can find in nature or in your heart. Let that field sing to you. What is a favorite song? Play it on repeat. Find your way to contribute to creating a better world in your unique way, a way that feels nourishing. I listen to "A Beautiful Noise" by Brandi Carlile and Alicia Keys. Another inspiring tune is Sara Bareilles's "Brave."

If your depression is overwhelming, reach out for help. Please talk to someone. You may think that because you are "so smart," you should not need help, but that's not true. Okay? I have worked with many therapists and other therapeutic practitioners along the way, and it has made all the difference.

"

The odd and magical
combination of things
that you love is exactly
what they need here.

You Loved the Teachers
Who Were Enthusiastic about Teaching—
You Did Not Love the Teachers Who Told
You Not to Read Ahead

RFMs can feel frustrated in school because the pace is slow, there is so much repetition, and you're not learning anything new. You may have been excited when you started school but were disappointed and then angry and resentful. On the other hand, you may have found school a safe haven from a difficult home life, or you fondly remember teachers who appreciated you and nourished your curiosity.

If you had a teacher you remember because they loved your endless questions and even your corrections of their errors, write a thank you letter to them. What are you grateful for? What did they do that made a difference in your life? Consider finding them online and emailing them your note. I have heard from former students, and it has been so gratifying. Teachers often don't know if they made an impact or not, and your note might mean the world to them.

If you recall difficult and traumatizing experiences, I don't recommend that you find those teachers online and tell them how they harmed you. However, it could be therapeutic to write a letter where you tell them off but don't send it. Write another letter to your child self, telling them how sad you are that they went through that. Correct any inaccurate beliefs they carry that resulted from their experiences in school. You may need to think about that for a while. What distorted beliefs about yourself resulted from your schooling? Did you decide you were not very smart? Did you reject your enthusiasm for learning and hide your curiosity even from yourself? If you were bullied by kids or teachers, tell your child self how unfair and hurtful that was. Let your child self write a letter to the bullies.

If you were redesigning the education system in your town, state, or country, how would you do it? Make a plan for how children learn and teachers teach in a way that meets everyone's needs. Make it your ideal school. What is the job description for the teachers? What does a day look like? Don't worry about what is realistic or pragmatic. Tell the story of your life in that school. How do you feel? Describe your ideal teacher. Let that teacher see who you really are, and write their evaluation of your true self. Let any emotions you feel rise up and release. If your ideas make sense and you have connections to local school administrators or a teacher friend, or you are a teacher, which ones might actually be implemented?

Time to Let the
Other Kids Feel Bad

Were you told to hide your abilities because the other children would feel bad about themselves? Were you told to downplay your achievements? Did you pretend your grades were lower than they actually were to avoid the bullies? Gifted kids often learn how to dumb themselves down from an early age. It's time to come out of hiding.

Make a list of your strengths, achievements, accomplishments, traits, and values. What activities nourish you? Include those. Go back to your early years. Who were you? Were you kindhearted? Helping others? Did you learn quickly and love reading? Were you looking out for grasshoppers and ants? Did you win the spelling bees or debate tournaments? How did others describe your strengths? Do not be modest, as no one has to see this list but you. What are the traits you're hiding because they have been rejected by others? Do you cry easily because of your tender heart? Do you rescue animals? Do you secretly love show tunes?

After you list your strengths, write about how hard (or easy) it was to do this. Were you told you needed to be humble or not show off? Were you told you were lucky and should not make the other kids feel bad? Write about that. Give yourself permission to notice and embrace your strengths.

This Is Your Brain on Giftedness

Draw a picture of your brain. What's going on in there? How would you picture the ideas, pathways, meanderings, questions, quests, feelings, thoughts, and doubts? Use many colors or media, or make it 3D. Let it be as detailed, odd, or unrealistic as you want. Maybe you have different departments. Maybe it extends into the rest of your body so you end up drawing your brain-mind-body. Is there a dance or a song that expresses this?

Write about your experience of this activity. Was it emotional? Freeing? Confusing? Would you show it to someone to help them understand you? Would you hide it?

Draw a flowchart or mind map that shows how you start with an idea and develop the other thoughts, ideas, sensations, and questions that come from that thought. You might need a large sheet of paper or several sheets or software. You might want to add colors and music, or you might dance it. Write about how it feels to see your experience of your ideas as a flowchart or a dance.

Maybe you have traits that seem to get in the way of the full functioning of your giftedness. Some of these are called "twice exceptionalities" or 2e. They can be ADHD, dyslexia, or autism, for example. Sometimes people consider anxiety or bipolar disorder 2e. Write about what it's like to be 2e. What are the ways you manage it? How would you draw your 2e traits in the picture of your brain-mind-body? There are websites for 2e: look for Bright and Quirky and With Understanding Comes Calm.

Strengthening Your Biodiversity and Resources

"

Just because you think deeply and often about the meaning, purpose, and quality of life on earth, does not mean you are a neurotic, self-absorbed, overthinking mess. And even if you are, on occasion, a neurotic, self-absorbed, overthinking mess, it is much better than being a neurotic, self-absorbed, underthinking mess.

Do You Worry Often about the Meaning of Life, the Future of the Planet, the Nature of Reality, and How to Create a More Compassionate World?

I t's hard not to be anxious these days. When you're perceptive and concerned about justice and the future, it's impossible to ignore circumstances and hard not to feel frightened.

This is a good opportunity to be in the present moment. I'm not good at this, but it helps to notice that in the present moment, I'm safe. I have enough food and water. There are no natural disasters in my town at the moment. Make a list of reminders. What are all the ways you're safe now? What are the tools you already use to calm yourself and soothe your nervous system? Add them to the list, and find a time every day to do at least one soothing activity.

Have you heard of the idea of sorting your anxieties into things you can control and things you cannot? Write what you cannot control on a piece of paper, and design a ritual where you hand that list over to a Higher Power, the Universe, Spirit, or God. Give over what you cannot control. Make a plan for changing some of the worries you can control. If it fits, design a ritual for those too, or use your intuitive abilities to create a magic spell. You may need to limit your exposure to the news. You may need to find allies or community.

If meditation is one of your tools, start your practice, and intentionally imagine you're taking yourself below the surface where the anxiety lives to a calmer, deeper, peaceful place in your body-mind. Find it, stay there, and feel the peace. Let your body tune in to this sensation slowly and deeply so it goes there more easily next time. Write about how it felt. Was it a struggle? Did you find the peaceful spot? What did it look like? How did it sound? Draw it, paint it, feel it.

Do you know about the Buddhist practice of tonglen? It helps me when I remember to do it! It is a meditative practice of what some call "welcoming the unwelcome." You breathe in all the anxiety of all beings everywhere and breathe out love to all. You might think it will increase your anxiety, but it will not. It is best explained by Pema Chodron, the popular Buddhist nun.

If you're worried about the future because of the climate crisis, look for the folks taking action. Mary DeMocker wrote a book for families called *The Parent's Guide to Climate Revolution.* Read *Generation Dread* by Britt Wray, or join one of the many climate crisis organizations. You may be upset by the many forms of injustice in the world. A few resources include the Southern Poverty Law Center, March for Our Lives, Van Jones, Resmaa Menakem, Glennon Doyle, Krista Tippett, Bryan Stevenson, and Jon Stewart.

Know that inner work and finding your authentic voice are powerful ways to help create a more compassionate world. Books that describe the importance of inner work combined with outer work are *Radical Regeneration: Sacred Activism and the Renewal of the World* by Andrew Harvey and Carolyn Baker and *Emergent Strategy* by adrienne maree brown.

Start a list of questions. What do you wonder about? What do you want to know? What are you worried about? Consider creating a journal that's full of questions. The rainforest-minded are often filled with questions. What would your questions look like as an art piece? What about a poem that's all questions?

Imagine what a beautiful future world would look like. You don't need to be realistic or practical. Write or draw or collage a vision of the best of humanity coming together in love and unity, evolving into a higher consciousness and a different way of living. Dream big without limits. See it happening. Notice how you feel. Let yourself tune in to what shamans call non-ordinary reality, and ask for the help of the invisible world. Taste, smell, and see this future. Read Patricia Albere's book, *Evolutionary Relationships,* and join her group, the Evolutionary Collective.

"

You may have been told how smart
you were over and over but with no
understanding of what that meant
or no support for your sensitivities
or emotional needs—just enormous
pressure to win, achieve, and be
the best.

Are You Flummoxed by
Your Multitudes?

You probably think that because you have so many interests, projects, job experiences, and books piled up by the bed that you don't attend to any of them in-depth. Some days, you may feel like a flighty, shallow, unserious time waster. I'm here to testify that you're not that. If you closely examine those interests, projects, career paths, and books, you find depth, complexity, and, in many cases, mastery. You may not realize this because you know how much deeper you could go, but if you compare your productions to those of less rainforest-y souls, you would see what I mean. You're probably evaluating your work from a gifted-level perspective. If you see it from a more general perspective, it would be high quality or even extraordinary.

It would be impossible to list all your interests or to organize your projects into some sort of linear, sequential, chronological structure, so what do you do? The main thing is to stop pathologizing your multipotentiality and see it as a strength, a natural trait of your rainforest mind. That will take you a long way. Stop trying to deny your divergent, creative, random-thinker self.

Get another journal devoted to your multipotentiality. Use it to record all your wild ideas—the ones you mean to dive into and the ones you don't. Chances are there's not enough time in a day/year/life to actualize all your ideas, but at least you can keep them cozy in your "Journal for the Divergent Random Creative Anti-Linear Multipotentialite."

How might you explain this to others? What do you say when they ask, "What do you do?" How do you explain all your different jobs and projects? Can you say you're a divergent random analytical creative (DRAC) or a nonlinear multipotentialite? Maybe you can say artist or entrepreneur, or just say you have a rainforest mind and show them the quiz.

Write about how difficult this is. Let out your frustrations.

There will be many projects, careers, and events that you experience over your lifetime, but what are the things you want to do but have to let go of? Write a goodbye letter to them or an obituary. What has to die so that you might live? You may have to grieve for the many projects you will not do, places you will not go, or people you will not be. Let yourself feel the losses even if no one understands because all they see is how much you have accomplished. If you want to find other multipotentialites, look online for Emilie Wapnick's website and her Puttyverse.

Finding Your Purpose(s)

There's no time to waste. You're here for a reason. Time to figure it out and get on with it—no more lollygagging, no more dillydallying, no more procrastination. The planet needs you to be who you're meant to be. I'm writing this book to get you there, and I know you have dreamed about it. You have longed for your purpose(s) to show you the way, but obstacles fell in your path and convinced you that there's plenty of time, you're meant to stay small and insignificant, or you're powerless because the changes required are impossible.

The good news is your purpose(s) is related to the things you love best. The projects where you lose track of time and forget to eat. The activities that make your heart sing. Your passions. Your creativity.

I realize you need to be practical if you're financially supporting yourself and a family, so keep that in mind. Your purpose(s) may or may not be connected to your income, but they do need to give your life meaning and a certain modicum of joy. It doesn't have to be big, bold, and visible. It might be subtle, quiet, and discreet, but it needs to include your rainforest strengths. What are they there for if not to lead you to yourself, your intuition, and your influence on the planet?

Start a mind map. Put "Purpose(s)" in the middle of the page, and go at it. Don't think too much. What comes to mind? Don't be practical or logical. Make it the largest, most complex mind map ever known. If you don't want to draw it by hand, find a mind map app. Go a little crazy. This is the beginning. When you're exhausted, stop and go back to it later. Use colored pencils/pens to emphasize your favorite ideas. See if a plan starts to emerge. If you get anxious or overwhelmed, do the other exercises in this book, and come back to this one when you have sorted out more of yourself.

You might have a sense of purpose but are afraid to shine, to show your full self. Maybe you fear success. Perhaps you carry memories of being burned at the stake, so being noticed is not appealing! Write about this. Have conversations with the parts of you that want to stay small. Examine their fears, validate their feelings, and find out what they need to feel safe. Write a story about how you conquered those fears and became a light to the world.

Again, you may need more time to work on this. It's a big deal. If you're not feeling particularly playful or inspired, go to a different page and come back later. Put on your emotional support sweater and get a cup of tea or a bowl of soup.

Do People Tell You to Stop Overthinking When You Wish They Would Stop Underthinking?

It's possible that anyone who is highly sensitive might be overwhelmed by others' emotions or behaviors or the disturbing sides of human nature. It's less common for the average person to feel underwhelmed in life, and this might be more unique to you. Your active, multidimensional brain-mind-heart-soul-spirit is often moving faster and deeper than those around you. You may often be waiting for others to catch up, and this can lead to lots of moments of underwhelm. See? It's not even a word because most people don't experience it, but it definitely exists in your dictionary.

Let yourself vent your frustrations in writing—your anger, rage, grief, and desperation at the mediocre, the mundane, and the wanton stupidity that you bump into all the time, everywhere. Don't censor yourself. No one needs to see it. This is important.

You're not alone in your exhaustion with the dumbfuckery. It can help to write or draw or dance your rage. Don't believe the people who tell you to repress the "negative" and just have positive thoughts. We call that "toxic positivity." Whatever you call it, there's a place for all the emotions, all the parts of you, all your multitudes. Expressing your sadness, frustration, anger, and despair in writing, in therapy, with a close friend, or with your trusty pup Henry is necessary for your well-being. It won't make more of it or bring you bad juju. It will be a healthy release, a chance to shift or move a thorny problem or obstacle, and open a door to new insight and expression.

You Can't Be Smarter
Than Your Parents and Teachers

Were you identified early as gifted? What was it like being seen as the gifted kid? Were you worried that you would disappoint parents and teachers if you didn't achieve according to their expectations? To your expectations? Do you still feel that pressure?

Maybe you weren't seen as gifted because of racism in your school or your unwillingness to conform. Perhaps you were seen as the athletic one and your sibling was labeled the smart one. Perhaps there was abuse or neglect in your family, and you had to figure out how to survive. Maybe no one paid attention to who you actually were.

Write a letter to that gifted child, and let them know that you see how smart, sensitive, or lonely they were. If you haven't already, design a way to meet regularly with this child and build a loving connection.

Are you afraid of failure? Terrified? Do you see even a small mistake as a failure? Describe situations where this happens. How did this start? How old were you when you started to get anxious about mistakes? It's often the result of parents and teachers overreacting to your early achievements, verbal abilities, and youthful curiosity. Write a letter to the younger you about this too. (We've talked about failure before, but this is important enough to mention again!)

All this talk about giftedness can stir up your impostor syndrome. Am I right? You can agree you have a rainforest mind, but gifted? Maybe not, and this may be because of all kinds of reasons. You know how much you don't know, or you think everyone must know what you know. Things come easily, but you never thought that was giftedness. You got good grades in school but said it was because the work was easy or the teacher liked you. You didn't score well on tests. You knew people who were *really* gifted. You were told not to get a swelled head or make the other kids feel bad. You could not be smarter than your parents and teachers.

I had a student tell me how disappointed he was with a mentor in high school. He had looked up to the mentor for a long time but realized the mentor was not as intelligent or insightful as he thought. Other adults disappointed him as well when he experienced their questionable ethics or complacency. When his own intelligence surpassed that of many of the adults he knew, it created a real conflict. Have you felt this disappointment and confusion?

Write about what it was like to have more capacity or success than your mentors, teachers, and/or parents. Write about your disappointment.

You may be looking for a mentor who can teach or guide you in your quest to learn everything. I recommend finding your Pips—as in, your backup singers. (You may have read about this on my blog, but it's worth restating. Years ago, there was a popular musical group called Gladys Knight and the Pips.) Can you imagine yourself in a band with four Pips as your support team? Visualize them, and create a playlist. They can be your backup until you find a mentor in real life. You may keep them around regardless. They might be authors, artists, musicians, people you have never met, or folks who are not alive.

"

Just because simple decisions
are almost impossible because
you wonder about the implications,
the variables, the variables within
the variables, and the impact of said
decisions, and you pressure yourself
to always be right, it doesn't mean
you're not as smart as everyone
says you are.

No-Pressure Success

There is a particular conflict that's unique to RFMs. On the one hand, you care deeply about the planet and the living beings on it. You want to help, to make a difference somewhere, somehow. You may want to have a significant impact in the world. At the same time, you may have felt pressure to be a high achiever from an early age because of how your parents, teachers, and others reacted to your intelligence. You were told how you would accomplish great things because you were so smart. Over the years, you hid or minimized your abilities. You may have given up and become depressed because the expectations were too great.

Write about what you remember about the early pressures. It's important to understand the reasons for this conflict so you can unravel it and decide for yourself what achievement looks like for you.

How do you define achievement and success? If you were to design a course called "No-Pressure Success for Smart People," what would the curriculum and the important points be? The homework assignments?

How might you rewrite the messages you received? What did you wish your parents had said and done? How might they have encouraged you without the pressure? Make a list of statements you wish you had heard. For example:

"I see how kind you are to the other children."

"I enjoy reading your stories—tell me more about this character."

"Tell me about your dreams, hopes, and fears."

"I'm glad you enjoy playing this game and what a good sport you are when you don't win. It can be hard to lose the game; you may feel sad or like something is wrong with you. Can you tell me how you feel? Everyone has wins and losses, and this is part of life. I can help you learn how to manage your feelings when you lose. It's normal for everyone, even gifted kids, to have strengths and weaknesses."

Time to Let Your Hair Unravel

When you grow up in a dysfunctional family, you may end up with patterns, beliefs, and needs that were good coping strategies then but are no longer useful. One of mine has been the need to be in control and able to leave a place at a moment's notice. When I feel trapped, well, it isn't pretty. We are often criticized for our *control issues*, but they're usually there for a good reason. It's a long, in-depth process to identify and begin to let go of the patterns that developed. Therapy is often important if there was abuse/trauma in the family.

Do you notice that you need control in certain situations? Does that need cause problems in your relationships? Write a "Woman/Man/Person Who" story describing your need to control, and see if you can gain some insight. Start with "Once upon a time, there was a person who…" Describe the issue, stay open, and let the story write itself. Consider adding humor. Keep writing until you feel relief or find a solution. This will raise your awareness and bring self-compassion to the situation. There are many examples of this technique in my journal entries in the back of this book.

Write a story in the third person describing the life you wish you had had. Tell the story of your life, and if your childhood was traumatic, end this version with a rescue. Maybe you were saved by Wonder Woman or Spiderman or a wise old grandma appeared. Maybe you turned into Wonder Woman or Spiderman yourself. After you complete the story, let it enter your brain/body and shift some neurons around.

"

Your mind palace may not be
appreciated by the masses.
Don't let that stop you.
Find the people who are ready
for you. Who love you for you.

The G Word

D o you still have trouble admitting you're gifted? Do you still mumble the word in conversation or not mention it at all? It can be hard to know what to tell others about your giftedness. Even if you get comfortable with the word, others may still react negatively if you use it. Sadly, people may think you're saying you are better than them or smarter, and no surprise, they typically don't want to hear that. I suggest that instead of using the G word, describe your specific traits. You might say, "I have a lot of interests and I love learning new things" or "I'm quite curious. I'm very sensitive to smells, sounds, and other people's emotions." These are more specific and more descriptive. You can use the quiz at the beginning of this book to help others understand you or you might create your own quiz.

Make a list of all the reasons you are *not* gifted. Do you know people who are smarter? Did you do poorly in school? Do you forget where you parked your car? Are you anxious when tests are timed? Do multiple-choice tests stump you because you can argue why all the choices might be correct, depending on the circumstances? Now, make a list of all the signs that you *are* gifted, including some of those same reasons! (Be sure to look for the documentary film, *The G Word,* produced and directed by Marc Smolowitz, released, hopefully, in 2024.)

Celebrating Your Resilience, Exuberance, and Regeneration

"

You have peculiar sensitivities,
unruly anxieties, and effervescent
expectations.

Are You Searching for the Person Who Can Keep Up with You or Even Surpass You?

Finding other RFMs can be difficult. It's the number one issue I hear about from clients and readers, but RFMs are out there! Who else is buying my books? If I was younger and had more energy, I might start an RFM friend/dating service or Facebook group. You all need to find each other, but since I'm probably older than your parents, I'll be keeping it simple.

When you know and accept who you are in your layered, tangled, exuberant complexity, more appropriate people start showing up in your life. Of course, you need to be active in some form to run into people, but if you're introverted and living during a pandemic, this might be a challenge. There are many online groups you can join if in-person life feels too overwhelming. These days, if you search for something you're interested in, you might find a local or international group to join. There is always a Silent Book Club and the Argentine tango.

Another idea is to create a career that attracts RFMs. That's what I did, and it's working beautifully. There is certainly a need for therapists who understand gifted souls, and coaching is popular now. With my blog, I hear from RFMs all over the world. It's thrilling. If I can do it, so can you!

Imagine yourself in a job/career that you love and that attracts smart, sensitive people. Make notes of the possibilities. Get creative. Don't limit yourself. If you're already doing it, write about that. How does it feel? If you need ideas on how to craft a career path, try the career guides by Barbara Sher, especially *Refuse to Choose,* or Emilie Wapnick's *How to Be Everything: A Guide for Those Who (Still) Don't Know What They Want to Be When They Grow Up.*

How might you expand your friend circle? What activities allow you to meet new people? Make a list. If you need to, come up with ways to introduce yourself to someone and suggest a meeting for tea or coffee.

Describe your ideal mentor. What are they like? What are their interests and abilities? How do they help you? Where do they live? Have a conversation with them here until you find them in real life.

Letters to My Future Partner

As of this writing, I have been happily single for many years. I have been in two significant partnerships (no kids) with lots of years productively and contentedly on my own. I now want to find a partner for this last act. I have a sense it's time for me to join with a male companion to learn about partner love and collaborate on creating a more compassionate world. There are many books about finding a partner, and the ones I have liked are *Calling in 'The One'* by Katherine Woodward Thomas and *If the Buddha Dated: A Handbook for Finding Love on a Spiritual Path* by Charlotte Kasl.

As I have said many times, finding other RFMs is not easy, for friendships or partnering. But using your creativity and intuition just might open the right doors.

Tap into the magic that is in and around you. Write a letter to a future mate, telling them about yourself. Take your time, and think about what's important to you. Do your best to be yourself and show who you really are through your letter. Be funny or serious or tender or weird. Be YOU. Poems, stories, drawings, collages, or mathematical equations are possible formats. Perhaps you will sense that you need to write a series of letters. Trust your intuition on this. Feel into the experience of knowing this person. Use all your senses to imagine their presence. Give the letter(s) to your person when they show up.

Is Your Big, Soft, Lonely Heart Breaking on a Regular Basis?

What is love? What kinds of love exist in life? English is so limited in describing love.

If you speak a language in addition to English, do you have many words for love? Write them down, and write about how you experience or don't experience love. Can you make up English words that mean love to you? Write the new words and their definitions. Paint them.

How are you loved? How do you love? Who do you love? Design/draw an image that represents LOVE in your life. See the varied and creative ways you experience it. Do you give and receive love to and from animals? Plants? God? Angels? Trees? Children? Family? Friends? Teachers? Coworkers? Bloggers? Writers? Artists? Musicians? Books? Dance? Nephews? Nieces? Grandkids?

Write an "Ode to Love." Start a book of love poems.

If you're looking for partner love, write a story to explore what might be in the way. Use my "The Woman/Man/Person Who" model to get started. Start with "Once there was a person who…" and describe the issue in the third person without knowing where it will lead. Trust the process. Add humor if you can.

"

Give yourself permission to be
deeply introspective your whole darned life.

Are You a Little Spooked by the Accuracy of Your Premonitions?

You may have witch-y, wizard-y tendencies. Maybe you have premonitions, or you're a healer, mystic, or channeler, or you have psychic abilities. Perhaps you dabble in the esoteric arts, metaphysics, ritual, and ceremony.

One way to think about this is that your capacity for intuition is large. If there was an IQ test just for this, you would be in the fourth, fifth, whatever standard deviation. Interesting word, deviation—it puts a positive light on the word *deviant*, doesn't it? What is it like for you? This might be another aspect of your personhood that you're reluctant to reveal and probably for good reason. How do you approach your family or friends? You may pick up the subtle cues that the rest of us miss. This is one of your strengths, but it may feel lonely, and on some days you may feel crazy. You're not crazy.

Make a list of the career paths/jobs where these skills would be useful. What about your intuition might be helpful at your job or with your family? Describe it. Do you need to develop these skills or feel more acceptance of them? Write about your ambivalence.

If you're hiding your abilities, think about the family members and friends who need to know this about you and are safe to tell. Write down some ways you might tell them about your abilities where they can hear about them. They may already have some idea and feel relieved that you finally brought this up.

Your intuition may be directly related to your spirituality (more on that later). Start keeping track of the moments when you get intuitive insight. Write them down. When you experience a synchronicity, keep a list. Make a page of intuitions and synchronicities. Get a tarot reading and/or study tarot. Let someone read your astrology chart and/or study it yourself. Read about shamanism, and learn how to journey. Read about near-death experiences and channeling. Anita Moorjani's work might be a good place to start. You may want to find an intuitive who could be a mentor or a friend.

My Mission Is to Help You
Find Your Mission

You've probably figured out by now that my mission is to help you find your mission so you can have a positive impact on yourself, your family, your community, and the planet. Imagine if all rainforest-minded humans on earth were self-confident, free from traumatic family-ancestral experiences, painful schooling memories, and inaccurate beliefs, could actualize their paths to personal transformation, and could transform humankind to a higher level of evolution! It's not too late for you or the planet.

In my experience, there are two main paths to improve life on earth: the inner and the outer. The inner path is the one you are on now. Reading and writing here with me and in other places. Exploring the depths of your psyche. Healing trauma. Gaining insight into your family patterns. Grieving for your unlived life. Waking up. Walking through the dark night of the soul. Setting boundaries with toxic family members and friends. Feeling your power and rediscovering your creativity.

The outer path might be trickier. You may have felt pressure all your life to achieve "greatness" because of your advanced abilities. My suggestion that you have an impact on the planet might trigger resentment, anger, or anxiety. I understand. I want you to get out from under the rubble of trauma, expectations, bullying, boredom, and fear, and shine your particular gorgeous light. You may have seen this quote from Van Jones on my blog: "Humanity's most consequential decade is now upon us. Your permission to play small has been permanently revoked."

I'm putting a little pressure on you, but it's not pressure to be someone you are not, win all the prizes, or climb the corporate ladder. It's support to find out who you are and what you are here to do.

What if you start with a mind map? Put your name in the middle with the question "Who am I?" Go crazy with possible answers, big and small, obvious and subtle. Use an app if you prefer. Include who you were when you were younger and who you will be when you're older. Pick something that feels impossible, and write a plan on how to get there. Be creative and impractical. See what you find.

If you're in a poetic mood, write an ode to or from your future self. Read it out loud, and then feel your future self in your body. Notice where your future self lives. Breathe into that place and feel it expand. Use as many senses as you can to tune in to your future self and receive messages.

Write a eulogy that will be read at your memorial service.

Write a screenplay where the future is a world of loving, evolved humans who live in peace and have respect for each other and all life on earth. Describe how they came together to stop the climate crisis and end injustice.

"

Getting your intellectual and
creative needs met will not only
lift some of your depression and
ease some of your anxiety. It might
be the foundation and inspiration for
your paths to your greater self, your
stronger voice, more cool solutions,
and, perhaps, a better world.

Tango Lessons

R FMs often have well-developed cognitive abilities, but the connection to their physical self might be less developed. How do you take care of your body? Do you participate in sports? Regular exercise? Dance? Yoga? Movement? How aware are you of your physical needs? Can you get into a flow state with your work and forget to eat? Have you had trauma that affected your comfort in your body?

Write about your connection with your body. How might you strengthen it? Complete the sentences

I'm grateful to my body for… _____

_____

_____

and

I could be kinder to my body if I… _____

_____

_____

See your body as an integral part of your rainforest mind. Where in your body does your intelligence live? Your sensitivity? Intuition? Let your body tell you in a meditation or written dialogue with it. Notice how it feels to tune in this way. Take your time. Write/draw what you notice. It may stir up uncomfortable memories. If this feels overwhelming, take a breath, stop, and move on to something else. If there is trauma in your past, consider contacting a therapist. You have a right to find support for your inner work. It's important to know when you need a professional guide.

When I started dancing the Argentine tango, I had to learn to feel my body in a way I never had before. To learn what it meant to bring my energy down into my legs and connect with the floor. To feel physically strong, to move with grace. To feel my body joined with another body so I could follow my partner's moves and feel the power and joy of being unified with another human. For several years, it was my therapy. It changed me. I recommend it.

What events have deepened your experience of your body? Write about them. How might you integrate your experience in the physical realm with your intellectual self? Your spiritual self? In addition to dance, consider yoga, working with clay, quilting, gardening, or playing an instrument. What else comes to mind? Imagine that your deeper body connection will guide you to more loving relationships and your particular way to contribute to creating a better world.

Never Too Late

You may think you're too old to change or to find a new job or career path. You may think you're too old to make an impact on the world. You're forty-two. Am I right?

If you have been reading my blog for a while, you know what I'm about to say. My sixties were my most productive decade. Sixties, and I was no slouch before that. I'm now starting my seventies and expect this decade to be the best yet. I've built a following, and that will only grow. (Your love notes sustain me!) I'm more confident than ever about what I have to share, and I feel more urgency to get it out there.

My dears, life gets better. Of course, you need to take care of your health, and that includes your mental health. I've been a client in therapy since I was thirty-one. I've worked with a number of psychotherapists over the years and participated in groups, classes, and many different forms of healing. The inner work has kept my body healthier.

Our bodies hold our trauma, so addressing early abuse, neglect, and other issues will help you heal the past, build confidence, and find meaning and purpose. It will also contribute to your physical well-being.

Tune in to your body. In a meditation, notice where there is tension or what feels like a block or obstacle. Give the tension a voice, and see what it has to tell you. Write its response. This might be intense and could require a professional if it feels overwhelming.

Picture your future self in five years, ten years, or more. What do you want to ask your future self? Ask, and then write the response. Take your time. It might not come easily at first, but this is important. Build an ongoing relationship with your future self for guidance and inspiration.

"

Just because you were told
that you must live up to your great
potential doesn't mean you have
to be the best whatever who ever
lived and win all the awards before
you're thirty. Choose yourself
over your potential.

Are You Soothed by Conversations with Trees, Rivers, and Spiritual Guides?

have mentioned your intuition, your knowings, your witchy wizardy proclivities. These often lead to a unique spirituality. You might follow a certain religion or have been raised with a set of religious beliefs. I find many RFMs seek something beyond traditional structures. In my experience, they are often more aligned with a mysticism, meditation, yoga, Buddhist-type beliefs, earth-centered spirituality, or shamanism. Many of my clients have their spiritual moments in nature and feel a higher power among trees or by rivers. You might be aligned with a particular religion and also feel a deep connection in nature. You might not see yourself as spiritual, but you resonate with the awesomeness of the natural world, how everything is connected, or the beauty of science.

Bring your journal with you to a cozy spot in nature. Get quiet, and notice your connection. Perhaps someone is speaking to you. Perhaps it's a tree, the river, or a raven. Write what you hear or feel, or draw what you see. Imagine this is spiritual guidance around you and inside you. Start a regular meeting with this guidance to deepen your connection and experience the wisdom. Trust it. You're not making it up. This is real.

Give yourself permission to go more deeply into your intuitive/spiritual skills and develop them. Write prayers or ask your network of spiritual guides for ways to navigate in this world. Write their responses. Build a relationship with your intuition or spiritual guidance.

Gather special objects that have meaning to you. Build an altar that represents your spiritual connections, and place it in a special location in your home. You might add photos of yourself at various ages to honor and protect your younger selves.

No Regrets

What do you think about aging? Are you still young and not thinking about it? Do you have family members with illnesses or age-related maladies that you are caring for? Are you, like me, reaching an age where you can no longer pretend you have all the time in the world?

Write about how your body is responding to aging. Are you anxious about the future and your mental and physical health? Design a preventive maintenance program that includes the steps to prepare for a long, healthy, fulfilling life. I recommend acupuncture with a skilled practitioner and lots of therapy! If you're dealing with illness or physical limitations now, how might you be kind to yourself and find nourishment? Do you have a loving pet, a partner who you can lean on more, or a hobby you have always wanted to explore? Use an art form such as collage or songwriting to gently stretch your boundaries. Don't wait for permission or retirement.

Make a list of all the things you want to do before you die—a No Regrets list (otherwise known as a Bucket List). Write your advice to younger versions of yourself or to yourself now. If you want to have no regrets when you die, what do you have to think, feel, say, and do now? Write about these in the form of a plan. You can get detailed, if that appeals to you.

Write as if you're ninety and attending a celebration of your life. Design the event. Where is it held? Is there food? Music? Dancing? Who is there? What are people saying about you? What are you proud of? Notice there is a display of your accomplishments—what do you see? What are people grateful for? If you have photos available, create a photo montage or photo essay.

Write a letter to yourself detailing your gratitude for your courage and willingness to travel on this revealing, strenuous, enlightening, challenging, magnificent
journaling journey.

My Journal Entries

"

Some days all we can do is
screech, scream, groan, moan, complain,
yelp, cry, and roar. With abandon.

wanted to include examples from my journals to help you see how I grapple with some of these topics. As I gathered them, I realized that my more recent approaches are not particularly varied as compared to the options such as drawing, designing, dancing, dialoguing, or ritual-making that I suggest! I write mostly longer, slightly humorous stories these days. Even though I have kept journals for many years and used a variety of techniques, I did not want to share older, dated entries here, so you will read several stories in a similar format. My purpose is not to demonstrate the different techniques but to show you more of me and join you in your vulnerability. To let you know you're not alone. Together, we are growing, healing, and building our passionate, powerful, and purposeful lives.

One journal entry at a time.

PLEASE NOTE

You'll notice I preface many of my entries with: "The Woman Who…," as I identify as female. However, this could easily be changed to "The Person Who…" or "The Man Who…," as it applies to you.

The Woman Who Thought She Was Morose and Sullen but Was Really Sweet, Bighearted, Loving, Funny, Smart, Sensitive, and a General Goofball

Once there was a woman who, as a child, was told she was just like her father. This was not good. This was not helpful. It was also not true, but she believed it. Her father was sullen, mean, and creepy. Dishonest. Perverted.

It could be said that this did not have a huge effect on her. After all, she did not believe she was mean, creepy, dishonest, or perverted, but she did believe she was sullen and morose. She believed it pretty much all the time. All those years. It did not help when her estrogen levels dropped, as you might imagine.

Truth be told, they were all sullen: her parents, grandparents, aunts, uncles, and ancestors. (Her father was the only one who was also mean, creepy, dishonest, and perverted.) Her sister was perky but only as a defense mechanism. Under the perky, she was scared. Now that I think of it, under all of it, they were all scared. Probably terrified, if you want to know the truth.

This news was useful. It put it all in perspective and gave her a more compassionate take on her family. Better to be sullen and morose than terrified, right? It seemed it was a practical answer to a difficult situation. You could say there was a lot to be scared of coming from her ancestral line, and chances were she didn't know the half of it.

What to do now? Clearly the woman did not enjoy being sullen and morose, but if she let go of sullen and morose, would she become fearful? Let's face it—the times were pretty darned scary, with ice caps melting and white supremacists running wild. She knew fear lurked in her neighborhood and leaked into her house fairly often. It was kind of a trifecta. Sullen. Morose. Scared. Oh my!

Well, what was her true nature? Who was she really? Even though sullen morosity and fear were her constant companions all these years, could she just say no? Could she realize her true nature—a sweet, bighearted, loving, funny, smart, sensitive goofball—and be that? Would it be that easy?

Easy, you say? Ha!! Not to worry. She had a billion years of therapy under her belt, so yes, she was ready now. It was easy *now*. It was time to take one more step and become who she was meant to be, who she always was. The truth was bubbling up in her heart. It was all there. It was always there. She just had to sweep off the last dust mites of morosity. Funny, when she looked around for fear, she didn't find it. Instead, she saw love coming at her. Love coming from her. Love under the table. Love in the refrigerator. Love through the internet. Love at the grocery store. Love appeared to be everywhere. It was almost too much to bear.

But she was used to being seen as too much. Too sensitive. Too dramatic. Too introspective. So too much love? She could bear it. She was certain of it.

The Woman Who Was a Walking Satellite Dish

Once there was a woman who was a walking cable TV satellite dish cell phone channeling phenomenon (CTVSDCPC). She had the largest capacity ever known to bring TV, radio, cell phone, and UFO communications through her body-cellular-brain and transmit them to her friends, lovers, acquaintances, neighbors, and anyone else in the vicinity. It was a vibration nightmare. Messages were coming through all the time from every direction. She was a royal wreck. It was impossible to sort out all the incoming calls, so she did what any smart, way overstimulated CTVSDCPC would do. She shut down the system, pulled the plugs, took down the towers, cut the cables, and turned off the radio. Ah. Silence. What a relief. Peace at last.

One day, the woman, happy and unaware in her turned-off state, met a most unusual man. He was amazing, kind, smart, funny, sensitive, creative, handy with a hammer, geeky with a computer, and awfully handsome. She was attracted to him and wanted to be his partner, but soon after they began dating, she saw there was something more. What was it? Every day when he visited her, she watched him. Something was familiar. Was it his love of trains and firetrucks? No. Was it his library of books on permaculture and gardening implements? No. Was it his entertaining stories about his days in the coast guard? No. It was a mystery.

One day, she noticed she was really attracted to him, and she wanted to throw herself at his feet, sob uncontrollably, and profess her vast love for him. But something was stopping the feeling from expressing itself, the feeling from feeling itself. Maybe her circuits were jammed, her heart wasn't big enough, or she wasn't the fascinating person she thought she was.

Then, it struck her. She remembered the day she shut down the system, pulled the plug, took down the towers, cut the cables, and turned off the radio. Gleesh. Was she going to have to become the CTVSDCPC again to experience this man in all his fabulous, deep effervescence? Oh no.

She stopped in her tracks, because she realized what was familiar. Oh yes, that's what she'd been noticing. This man had the same vibration nightmare, only he seemed to be handling it well. He even seemed to enjoy it for the most part and let it enhance his ability to be kind, smart, funny, sensitive, creative, handy with a hammer, geeky with a computer, and awfully handsome. Oh dear. Oh dear. What did this mean?

She sat for days, ruminating. What was the problem? Things were fine as they were. Just because she was unplugged didn't mean she couldn't enjoy this man and give him a fair slice of intense love. It was fine. No need to tune in and turn on. Even though he was receiving the latest and greatest communications from the stars and the land, it didn't mean she had to. She'd had it with that stuff. It made her crazy, gave her headaches, and distracted her from her ballroom dancing lessons. He liked her anyway. He loved her. She was fine vibrating at a nice even keel.

One day, she started to notice two important things. One, she was getting headaches every day and suspected that some vibrating communication from Pluto or Daffy Duck, or, God forbid, the center of the earth was banging on her head, trying to get in. Trying to get her to tune in and turn on again. Two, she wasn't able to connect as completely with her man. She would come and go. Feel the glow and then go numb, vibrationless, and unable to truly be with her man in all of his fascinating effervescence every darned minute and in the synergy that she knew was possible if they could allow their vibration nightmares together to become their flowing oceanic gyrating worldwide web of ecstatic love songs.

Oh bosh. Oh faplooi. What to do.

Hm. Synergistic oceanic gyrational love songs. Well, when you put it that way, how bad could it be? When she was the walking CTVS-DCPC phenomenon, she was alone, single, solitary. Maybe with her man, it could be a different experience. Together, they could figure out how to organize the deluge of incoming calls. Even though he wasn't the most orderly guy on the planet, he had a grounding cord that made it to the center of the earth. He could juggle many balls at one time and was good at list making. With his marvelous skills and her ability to dance and shriek and insist on the proper placement of objects in her home, they might make it.

She began to believe it was possible to open to the signals of the galaxies, earthly spirits, and CNN and not go psychotic. Not only that—perhaps, just perhaps, she and her man could hear the messages from the gods and help beings all over the planet feel their own oceanic gyrational love songs and begin to dance to them in ways never before possible.

Well then, okay, let the vibrations, gyrations, and elations begin.

When the Tango-Dancing Therapist Loved the Nature-Obsessed Neighbor from Hell

He was a die-hard camping, hiking, nature-loving Oregon hippie. He parked his truck on his overgrown lawn. Paraphernalia from long-gone construction projects was piled along the side of his house and scattered hither and thither in case he might need them in a year or five. I remember thinking the first time I drove up to his house that he was your typical neighbor from hell.

What was I doing with the neighbor from hell?

We met online. Even though his photos made him look dorky, I liked what he had to say. He read Annie Dillard. He was going to Idaho to take care of his mom after her hip replacement surgery. He was self-employed in the renewable energy field. Had raised two kids who made it to adulthood. Drove a Prius. In our email exchanges, he asked smart, complex questions and told fascinating stories about his adventures in the Arctic, all signs the man might be worth meeting.

The first meeting went well. He was much cuter than the photo. Tall, well built, articulate, smart, and sensitive. He did not smell like garlic. On our second date, he watched me dance. I had started taking Argentine tango lessons five years earlier. Craig was impressed, even though it was an unusual second date with me dancing with handsome men who were not him. He was a good sport about it, appreciating my talent.

I introduced him to my girlfriends, looking for their assessments.

Me: I don't know. He's kinda hippie-dippie. His house is super messy. I don't know if I'm ready for another relationship, and, anyway, he's probably a serial killer or codependent pothead with siblings who are in prison for insider trading.

Girlfriends: He has great social skills and a sense of humor. This could be fun. C'mon, there's no harm in trying. A serial killer probably wouldn't have a good relationship with his mother.

I decided to give it a try.

It was sweet.

But I am not a die-hard camping, hiking, nature-loving Oregon hippie. I thought I might become one with the right guy. Maybe not die-hard. Maybe not camping where there might be bears, cougars, raccoons, and no internet. I was an ardent environmentalist, so I thought I just needed a safe, kind soul to introduce me to the wonders of a rushing river, the mysteries of hiking in the forest, and the thrills of outdoor plumbing.

Craig tried. I remember one weekend in a comfortable yurt by a lake. He brought a solar cell thingy so we could have music. He supplied flashlights, delicious snacks, and a kayak built for two. I tried to enjoy myself.

He didn't give up. Months later, he bought a small trailer so we could stay at campgrounds with showers and restrooms. He cooked gourmet-ish meals and was upbeat and generous.

Sadly, it didn't work. I couldn't love it like he did. I couldn't even like it much. I was a failure at nature-loving, but there were other strengths I brought to the relationship.

For example, I was a success at psychotherapy loving.

I was a counselor, working with people healing from childhood trauma. I loved my job. It was such a privilege to guide people on their journeys to self-acceptance and self-actualization. I had also been a client in therapy. It was one of my core values: introspection and facing one's fears to heal yourself and create a better world. I was able to bring a good bit of self-awareness and compassion to the relationship. This could make up for my nature-loving deficit.

As I got to know Craig, it became clear that he had his own childhood trauma, but psychotherapy was not his thing. When it came to introspection or diving into the abyss, as I called it, or just looking under the rug, he would decline, change the subject, or play the nature card.

I would say: "Honey, I'm sorry your father was so critical. It sounds like he may have been an alcoholic. Therapy has been so helpful for me. I'm much more confident and less depressed. I can give you a few names of therapists you can try. Okay? It's so worth it."

He would say, "Nature is my therapist."

I knew there were many ways to self-actualize. Psychotherapy wasn't the answer for everyone, and nature could be such a healing place. Many of my clients found solace and even spirituality when they were connecting with the natural world, but for Craig, it was his solace and his excuse.

I would say, "Sweetie, if you don't want to do traditional therapy, how about meeting with my medical intuitive energy worker or my acupuncturist?"

He would say, "Nature is my therapist."

He was adamant in a nice guy, passive-aggressive kind of way. I had to admit he did try therapy a couple of times. He went to a weekend workshop. Spent a week at a nature-based vision quest program. He even saw my medical intuitive energy worker once. He tried, but he didn't love it like I did. Could not even like it much. He was a failure at psychotherapy loving.

As time passed, I started to see signs of trouble. Serious anxiety. Problems with his adult children. Unpaid taxes. Toxic friends. Vodka. Rooms in his house filled with old magazines, tools, gadgets, papers, and moth-eaten suits from his days in the tech world.

Like any good therapist, I ignored the signs. We bought a house together and planned a small remodel that turned into a big remodel. He was a capable self-made contractor, so he wanted to do it all himself, which took a lot of time. I stayed in my own house until it was mostly complete and then let my home, my little sanctuary, go. He didn't sell his own house and, lucky for me, left most of his clutter there but not his anxiety, unpaid taxes, or vodka.

Once we were living together, I noticed the garlic. He loved it. I had a thing about food smells on breath, especially garlic. If someone smelled like garlic, I immediately despised them. My therapist self knew that this is an overreaction, likely a bad memory from the past, but those olfactory triggers are hard to control. I started to eat garlic as a way to reduce the odor and manage my despising. It helped, and I tried not to hold it against him.

We grew closer in spite of our failures and differences. He kept his chaos contained to his office and the garage. I ate more garlic and bought gifts for his grandkids. He was my bodyguard when we visited my family. I befriended his mother when she needed a careful listener.

We were creating a good tango. We'd step on each other's toes occasionally but our hearts were in sync.

Then the music stopped.

One day, he told me it was over. He said he needed a partner who loved the outdoors as much as he did. Who could walk the beach for days. Who was intensely curious about the ocean floor and eager to spend weeks lost in the Oregon forest.

I was in shock. I had thought he was the one, that this was going to be my last and best relationship. I thought it was going well. He would take his trailer to the coast for a few days and enjoy nature on his own while I stayed home, saw clients, and blogged. I had started a blog about three months before the breakup. It was surprisingly satisfying, meaningful, and fun.

I thought we had worked out a good compromise. Apparently, we had not.

It wasn't easy for him to break up with me. I cried. He cried. He offered to move back to his old house until I found a place and we sold ours. Move out? Back to his old house? It took me some months to believe it was over and that I was being left—not for another woman but because he loved Mother Nature more than he loved me. That was weird, if you ask me, but he was not asking.

He moved back to his house, and I was alone.

I had support. Over the years, I had built a reliable family of girlfriends. My friends and my blog would get me through my grief.

For a long time, I felt lost and lonely. No one tracking me anymore. No one asking me annoyingly what my schedule was for the day. No funny stories of polar bears. No bodyguard for family visits.

But I did what I had to do. I went to therapy, and it occurred to me that Craig and I had very different basic needs. His was finding peace (and denial) in the beauty of the natural world. Mine was doing deep psychospiritual work to heal my past and live a life of meaning and purpose. Interestingly, we were both inept at participating in the other's greatest priority.

I began to wonder how we had lasted as long as we had, why I didn't run the other way when I first saw his neighbor-from-hell yard. Why he didn't run the other way when he heard I was a therapist. In spite of it all, I knew our partnering had not been a mistake.

As I continue to unpack the layers of my psyche, one thing is clear. I'm certain I want a partner who is willing to look under the rug. Who isn't afraid to do the deep dive into his abyss. Who wants to do the inner psychospiritual work to heal the past and live a courageous life of meaning and purpose.

To keep the music playing, our hearts in sync.

To tango, fearlessly, with me.

The Woman Who Surrendered

Once there was a woman who was fighting with herself. Well, she was looking for a way into her body. Well, she was alienated from living life on earth. Well, all the above. She had closed up access to her body since she came onto the planet as a way to avoid annihilation.

One day, she started to wonder if it might be a good idea to relocate her body and reenter, since she'd not only cut off access from outsiders but had excommunicated herself. Imagine that!

Unfortunately, she realized she had lost the key to her body and couldn't find the door even if she had the key. This was a problem. She hadn't realized that living in her head and leaving her body empty and unavailable for entry would result in particular problems like a depressed, zombie-like existence or a heart that was frozen and crusted over with sticky, gummy, disgusting debris so that she couldn't feel the love from a remarkable man or couldn't feel gratitude for her amazing life or couldn't feel appreciation for the abundant beauty all around her. Bummer. Really.

Realizing this dilemma, she tried to find the door back into her body. Even without the key, if she found the door, she could break it down and get in. She did all kinds of contortions to find it: joined a gym, consulted with mystics and magicians, meditated, got massaged and acupunctured, used drugs, indulged in her book-buying obsession, breathed, had sex with her adoring partner, wrote stories like this, ate chocolate fudge brownie ice cream, ruminated extensively, and bought hair care products from elite salons in New York City.

Nothing worked. Well, it all worked, but she was still at odds with the universe, or so it seemed.

She was bereft. This was no way to live. She'd managed this far but had gotten more depressed as time went on. The future looked bleak.

One day, after some serious self-deprecation, it dawned on her. *STOP TRYING. Surrender. Give up. Don't look for the door. Don't try to get back in. Find the benefits of staying out. Let your body stay boarded up and unused. Look at how extraordinarily well you've done without it. Why change that? Really, what are you thinking? Gratitude is over-rated. Love is unnecessary. Let go of this crazy New Age idea of being grounded. What the fuck.*

The woman started to shiver. A cold chill ran through her body. Her body? Really? Well, that was interesting. She could feel cold.

Hm. What if the real deal was that she did have access to her body all along? What if the door was already open, but she didn't realize it because it didn't feel like she thought it should? Maybe there wasn't a door, because it was not a house but a super highway or open road. Maybe her body was a Broadway musical. Maybe she'd been using the wrong metaphor all this time. She was looking for a key, a door, access to the house when she was an open book, a song, or a musical instrument. Words, vibrations, and music were her access points.

Maybe it was a matter of a new paradigm. A way many dissociated, disembodied darlings could accept themselves. What if there was a larger motif? Maybe some people could be oceans or mountains. She could imagine that possibility, but for now, she'd start by embodying *her* true nature, which appeared to be herself as a musical comedy, song and dance team. A vibrating, Tony award-winning extravaganza. She started to feel a song coming on. "Oh, what a beautiful morning" came spurting out from somewhere, maybe even her heart.

Single, Child-Free, Petless, and Loved

Life is kinda overwhelming. When I think about taking care of living things, I get nervous. A dog. A cat. A human. A philodendron. I don't know how people do it.

My evil twin says that many of them shouldn't be doing it—taking care of living things. Raising kids, for instance. Look at all the conflict around the world, and you can see clearly that many folks are screwing it up.

I am always overwhelmed. There are the obvious things: melting glaciers, hatred, ignorant politicians, poverty, angry Twitter posts, and hormone imbalances, for starters. The less obvious are leaf blowers, tacky architecture, garlic breath, bad hair days, and groups of more than one person. My temperament is a factor. I'm introverted, introspective, and sensitive, which others have called geeky, dramatic, and weird.

Considering my consistent state of overwhelm, I haven't done a bad job. Living, I mean. I've been in significant partnerships. I have sweet friends. I've danced the tango in Paris. And I have a career that I love. You can probably guess what it is. I'm a psychotherapist. It's the perfect career path for someone particularly sensitive to life, people, responsibility, and screwing up.

You could argue that my clients are living things that I'm responsible for, and you'd be partially correct, but there's a limit to the responsibility. It's different. Sure, I love my clients. We go on intimate journeys together. We learn about safety, trust, and self-acceptance. It's deeply nourishing, but I'm not folding their laundry or paying their college tuition. I'm not organizing their birthday parties. They aren't puking on me or demanding my car keys.

Due to my psychotherapeutic proclivities, sensitivity, introversion, and overwhelm, I've consciously chosen to be child-free and petless. Single has been fine too. I've always been fond of having control over my environment. It can be tricky if someone other than me is trying to cook or shriek or leave their dirty dishes hither and thither. I enjoy my solitude and like having the time to obsess when I want and how I want.

That said, the idea of a soul companion is appealing. The last one was a good one. He was smart, kind, and a great communicator. We had nine sweet years together, remodeled a house, and healed some of each other's old wounds. The relationship ended when it became clear that hiking in the wilderness, sleeping with spiders, and living without my laptop would never be my favorite thing. It ended when it became clear that examining and processing the deep-seated neuroses that were at the root of his anxiety and wheel-spinning would never be his favorite thing. We parted as friends after some crying. Okay, a lot of crying.

Luckily, before we split, I had the brilliant idea to start blogging. Becoming a blogger is surely what every single, child-free, petless person needs.

There is a loneliness factor in the single, child-free, and petless life. I hate to admit it, but it appears that humans need to feel that they belong somewhere and are loved. Imagine that. I suppose it's part of the human condition, and as much as I hesitate to say this, I suppose that I'm human.

Blogging serves many needs. I express my creativity and support others from the comfort of my peaceful home or at my favorite café. I have friends in Slovenia. At 3:00 a.m., when I can't sleep, someone "likes" me. I'm influential and don't have to deal with baggage fees. I talk to fascinating folks in Ireland and Brazil. People pay to hear my thoughts. My life is making a difference. I belong in the world and to myself. I'm loved.

Not too shabby.

Of course, blogging doesn't solve everything, so I have my team of practitioners. My acupuncturist, my Rolfer, my medical intuitive, my tango teacher, and my psychotherapist. I still need my hormone replacement therapy and my hair products.

Yes, there are lonely nights when I wonder if I should break down and get a philodendron. If a wonderful man who doesn't leave dirty dishes hither and thither were to come along, I'd be open.

Honestly? The single, child-free, petless life?

It's good. Very good.

The Woman Whose Hair Could Not Be Controlled

It was in her hair. The control. If she let her hair be free, all hell would break loose. If her hair was free, she couldn't hide. She'd walk into a room and people would notice her. She'd walk into a room, and people would be appalled at her bold, expressive, obnoxious, unruly hair. She'd walk into a room and people would ask her to be responsible for something.

Then what? Her safe, secure, smallish world might explode on her, shattering her melancholy, depressive, uneventful life. Who knows what might emerge from there? Surely something large, loud, slimy, and smelly that would be intolerable. At least her melancholy, depressive, uneventful life was not large, loud, slimy, or smelly. There was that.

She liked control. She. Loved. It. Who didn't? Anyone who grew up in any sort of moderately to severely dysfunctional family craved the sweetness of being out from under the fuckedupedness. Into one's own world, creating one's own path, away from the neediness, unspoken rage, and cold criticism. Even if one's own path led to fuckedupedness, it was your own fuckedupedness. She could live with that.

Except for the fact that her hair kept popping out of its containers. No matter the conditioners, gels, and paraben-free shampoos, the clips, braids, hats, avocado-banana-yogurt masks. Her hair could not be contained. It screeched LOOK AT ME at every turn. It cried I AM HERE. It yelped I'M A REBEL AND I'M PROUD.

Oh boy. What to do. What to do.

There was the obvious: cut it all off. (I'm kidding. That was not an option.) She could let it unravel and see what happened. It was possible she could maintain a modicum of control even with her obnoxious hair showing its true self. She had to admit that other people didn't see it as obnoxious. They seemed to like it. They even wanted it for themselves.

Maybe it was time. She wasn't getting any younger, but what if she was seen? What if people noticed? What if she claimed that she was alive, rebellious, and proud? What if her true self screeched I AM HERE? Would that be so bad? What if she came to love her control *and* her unruly hair? Maybe they could coexist.

Maybe she'd have *more* control if she let her hair go. Would that be possible? Had she been misguided all this time? Was there true control in no control? Was she getting too Buddhist? Maybe saying yes to her hair, she was saying yes to life. Perhaps there was room to expand, to grow, to evolve from her melancholy, depressive, uneventful life.

Perhaps her effervescent, expansive, evolving hair could lead the way.

Dear Future Boyfriend,

You'll need to know some things about me before you venture into my world, into the jungle that is my rainforest mind. I'll start with my head. I have a lot of hair. Massive amounts of exuberant, curling, ridiculous hair. I try to control it, but I'm unsuccessful. You might think this is a wonderful thing, but I'm warning you. Wildly untamed aspects of my psyche live in my hair.

Next, I'm very sensitive. This is good if you need me to be perceptive, insightful, generous, and kind. This is not good if you want to avoid dealing with the effects of your dysfunctional family of origin. If you like emotions, I'm your gal. Deep, intense, rich emotions. You'll be happy to know I have been in therapy for many years, so the rage is, well, negligible. It surfaces only in times of extreme stress, when I feel trapped, or when I run out of estrogen or hair products.

Like many of the rainforest-minded, I'm on a spiritual quest. I'm obsessed with living a heart-centered, magical, purposeful life. (You too?) I want to contribute something meaningful to our troubled planet and connect to a spirituality that I suspect is both inside me and around me. Unlike those who find their spirituality in religion or nature, my quest takes me other places.

I find my connection to the Mystery in more unusual ways. Once, while dancing the Argentine tango, I felt a spiritual message coming from under the dance floor. Yes, under the floor. It was a message of support and sweetness from what I imagine as the Big Love or, since you are probably a *Star Wars* fan, as The Force.

If that isn't odd enough, I also sing, but it's not what you think. Although I used to have a penchant for Broadway musicals, I now seem to be singing weird melodies channeled from distant galaxies. When we meet, I will demonstrate. Because you're my mate, it will all make sense in a compelling, metaphysical, rainforest-y way.

Oh, did I mention I'm a psychotherapist, seeking to change the world one dysfunctional family at a time?

There are normal things about me that I could share, and I will in future letters. I thought I would get my more, um, unique traits out of the way to be sure you know what you're getting into.

So that's me, Future Boyfriend. I'd like you to show up soon. I'm not getting any younger. We have work to do. Dances to dance. Songs to sing. Magic to make.

May the Big Love be with you.

The Woman Who Was Afraid of Partner Love

Once upon a time, there was a woman who had many fears. She was afraid of wildfires, climate catastrophes, pandemics, rats, homelessness, starvation, poverty, losing her mind, running out of hair gel, and public speaking. She acknowledged that her fears were reasonable and that many people had similar anxieties.

What made her unusual was that she was also afraid of love. Not just any old love. She was fine with friends and family loving her, with clients loving her. Fine with fans of her blog, books, and Instagram posts. This was fine, even great. It sustained her through the lonely, scary nights when she might ruminate over pending dry summers or rat invasions or supply chain catastrophes where her hair gel was stuck on boats in Thailand forever.

She was terrified of BIG LOVE with a partner. You know what I'm talking about. The sacred relationship kind of love. The love that overwhelms you with glee. The love that strips away all your defenses. The love that redefines and redesigns intimacy. The love that implodes your nervous system and rewires your brain.

You might say that BIG LOVE is a fantasy. It's only in the movies, so why worry about it? It exists only between you and divinity, or it exists only between you and your dog, Fido. In the real world, there's morning breath, irritability, attachment issues, drug-addicted children, and snoring. No need to get all bent out of shape. There is no BIG LOVE.

Well, that's a relief, she thought. What was she thinking? There was no such thing as BIG LOVE, so no need to get all tied up about it.

If it existed here and there in rare moments of awakening, who was she to think it would find her? She didn't want it anyway.

Or did she?

Then, suddenly, she remembered her destiny. She recalled that she had an assignment when she agreed to come to earth. It was tricky at the time because she knew the planet was in torment and upheaval, but she agreed to go to earth on one condition. Her guides would keep her safe and comfy throughout her life as she accomplished her tasks even though there would be chaos all around her. They would also give her the experience of BIG LOVE with a partner that some humans in bodies were able to experience, the kind of love that made life on earth worth it. That might even be the goal of life on planet earth: creating BIG LOVE between humans and spreading it around. (The spreading it around part was important. You wouldn't want to be selfish.) The agreement was real. She had signed a contract and everything. She remembered this with some trepidation and some hopefulness.

In that moment, she felt a shift. What was it? Was she suddenly ready for BIG LOVE? She checked in with her nervous system. It told her it could handle BIG LOVE. She would not implode, explode, disappear, or lose all her hair. She checked in with her heart. It was more than ready to expand, open, soften, and welcome her person. She checked in with her anxiety. It told her it was waiting for someone it could rely on who would join her in opening jars, roasting vegetables, and chasing away invading rodents. She checked in with her body. It said there was still a lot of sensual/sexual capacity waiting to be tapped. She checked in with her Spirit. This was exactly what her Spirit was waiting for, and she could not be more delighted. She checked in with her Soul, which was singing "Hallelujah." She even checked in with her ancestors who were all cheering, "Mazel tov."

Well, that sure sounded like a BIG YES to her. She would fulfill her destiny after all. Complete her contract. She and her man would become BIG LOVE and spread it all over the planet, as it was ordained very long ago.

Mazel tov indeed.

Tango Lessons

"Would you like to go salsa dancing with me on Friday?"

"Excuse me?" I said.

"Would you like to go salsa dancing?"

"Are you talking to me?"

He was gorgeous. He had that JFK Jr. handsomeness. I thought this was a joke. We were in a swing dance class. I didn't know him. I was forty-seven. He was, um, young.

We switched partners, and I was dancing with Farmer John, who smelled a little like the farm. The handsome young guy had moved to the next girl. Maybe he was asking her to go salsa dancing with him, too.

He came back around to me with that make-you-wanna-melt smile. "Salsa? Friday?"

How did he know I had been taking salsa lessons?

When the class ended, we talked. He was twenty-nine and a graduate student at the University of Oregon, having emigrated from Russia with his engineer parents when he was ten. He was getting business and psychology degrees and had recovered from a cancer scare when he was twenty-one. The mythologist Joseph Campbell was one of his heroes. I learned a lot about him quickly. I was a psychotherapist. I asked questions.

"Shall I pick you up on Friday, or do you want to pick me up?" he asked.

When I determined he was serious, I suggested we meet at the dance venue. I wasn't ready to get into a car with Alexander, the young, charming, drop-dead-gorgeous Russian-American.

Just so you know, I'm a feminist. I don't put much emphasis on looks. I don't care about such things. I'm evolved. Middle-aged, for heaven's sake. But his young, tall, dark handsomeness was impossible to ignore. Maybe because I was never the popular girl, the one who people noticed. I was the one with an ethnic look, curly haired and introverted, the anti-cheerleader. The beautiful boys never sought me out for salsa dancing.

He told me he had seen me dancing salsa a month ago. He had wanted to ask me to dance then, but I was talking with another young man (his roommate, it turned out), so he didn't want to intrude. Maybe I wanted to date his roommate, he thought.

Where had this guy come from? Was I dreaming him up? Maybe I was living in an alternate universe.

I had been divorced for about ten years and looking for a new hobby that would get me out into the world, meeting people. I tried ballroom dance classes: swing, salsa, and Argentine tango. I loved dancing and was pretty good at it. I was particularly fond of salsa and tango and had started taking tango lessons on Sunday afternoons. The tango was not easy to learn, but there were a couple of excellent teachers in my town, and the tango seemed to attract fascinating people: smart, sensitive, creative folks who were looking for a way to express themselves artistically while connecting with others in a safe yet intimate way.

I danced with Alexander that Friday night at the restaurant. It was thrilling. My heart was pounding. I left early because I didn't want to faint from the excitement of it all. That would have been embarrassing.

As it turned out, Alexander was also taking tango lessons. Sunday afternoons, tango classes were held downtown in a large, mirrored space with a shiny wood floor. We had a lesson for an hour and then practiced for the next hour. To dance well, I had to become more tuned in to my body. I had to feel my feet caressing the floor and move my energy down my legs versus up into my head where it usually lived. It was challenging, but the community was welcoming, and the dance was satisfying. I ended up dancing three to four times a week. It was intoxicating. The Argentine tango became my therapy.

Alexander and I built a friendship. We had a regular breakfast meeting on Saturday mornings. He would come to my home at 9:00 a.m. sharp for coffee and eggs and then stretch out on my too-small sofa to talk about Carl Jung, Joseph Campbell, and the roots of happiness. We practiced tango outside on my deck. He had been dancing longer than I had, so he made suggestions on how I might improve. He was an impatient teacher, but I didn't care.

As my dancing progressed, I noticed that men would watch me. The blond, thirty-something marine wasn't a dancer but was occasionally at the café where we danced on Tuesday nights. It seemed I had discovered an answer to aging well. No matter if you were the older, ethnic, curly haired, anti-cheerleader—dance well and you would be popular.

I remember dancing with a man closer to my age. Rick was a talented leader, playful, creative, and sensitive. The faster tangos were particularly fun. Being in sync with his musicality and his grounded body was exhilarating. One day, he stopped asking me to dance.

"Rick, I've noticed that you don't ask me to dance anymore and avoid my gaze when I try to ask you. Have I offended you?" I asked.

"Um, uh, well, um, uh, no. I, well, um, I might have mentioned to my girlfriend that I thought you were a passionate dancer," he replied.

"Oh. Oh. Okay. Good to know. Thanks for telling me."

It turned out his girlfriend thought I was too passionate. I missed Rick but was relieved I had not offended him, and I was grateful for the odd compliment.

Rick was a better tango dancer than Alexander, but with Alexander, there was a special electricity. We talked about the sexual attraction. Neither of us wanted to ruin what we had. Alexander was dating women closer to his age, which made sense to me. I wondered, though, if he stayed more superficial with the women he dated. Perhaps he and I were closer because we were not dating.

He said, "Let's put that sexual energy into the dance."

We did. Tango, it turned out, was better than sex.

There were times when Alexander disappeared and did not respond to calls. It was becoming clear that he struggled with depression. He could be temperamental and distant. His father died when he was sixteen, which the therapist in me suspected was a loss he had not processed. There was so much I did not know about his past. He started to miss some Saturday morning breakfasts but later showed up at a dance class or a milonga with his mesmerizing smile. When we danced, it was magic except for the times he felt like I was pulling on his neck or not following him perfectly, which happened when he was in a mood or when I was wanting more.

I admit I was not totally content with the arrangement. I was getting attached. I started writing bad poetry about our unusual pairing, journaling about my ambivalence and my desire.

He moved to Portland. He graduated and felt too stifled in our town. Portland, two hours north, would provide more opportunities for work contacts and dancing. We stayed in touch, and I went to Portland to dance a few times. He drove back to Eugene on occasion, but it wasn't the same. With the distance, it was easier for me to be rational about the knowledge that he was not boyfriend material.

He moved to Paris. Alexander needed the stimulation of a big city, a new language and culture, and French women. I realized he had always been restless in Oregon. He sent me postcards from France and seemed happier there. Periodically, he asked me to visit him in Paris. I considered it. Then he invited me to his wedding.

Veronika was French, beautiful, smart, and his age. Her hair was not curly. If they had cheerleaders in France, she probably was one in high school. Of course, he was marrying her.

I didn't go to the wedding. If I was going to take my introverted, travel-phobic self to Paris, it wasn't going to be when Alexander ignored me because he had better things to do like get married. I waited until his son, Mateo, was born.

He asked me again. "Come to Paris, Paulina" (his nickname for me).

"I don't know, Sandro (my nickname for him). Travel makes me nervous. If I go, can I count on you to pay attention and not leave me stranded somewhere?"

"I will not leave you stranded. We can dance tango along the Seine in the evening. It will be fun."

Tango? With Alexander? In Paris? Along the Seine?

I went to Paris.

During the eleven hours on the plane, I ruminated. I spoke only high school French. What if he wasn't at the airport when I arrived? He was not the most reliable guy. I mean, I hardly knew him. What if Veronika didn't like me? What if he was depressed the whole week? What if I forgot how to dance? What if I twisted my ankle, had an allergic reaction to escargot, did something culturally insensitive, or lost my hair gel?

My fears were unfounded. He was at the airport when I arrived, and Veronika was sweet and welcoming. They were kind hosts, and I managed to communicate while seeing the sites by smiling and saying *merci* a lot. I had never seen anything like Paris.

We went tango dancing along the Seine one night. I was intimidated and incredulous. I tried to keep my ethnic, curly haired, introverted self calm, but it was difficult when the French men spoke to me, holding me close. It took my breath away. They didn't seem to care that I wasn't popular or had no idea what they were saying.

Surely, this was an alternate universe.

It seemed I had discovered an answer to aging well—feeling attractive as I headed into later middle age. No matter if you were the ethnic, curly haired, anti-cheerleader—dance well and you would be popular.

You may even get to dance the tango in Paris.

Dear Spiritual Guides,

I haven't talked to you in a long time. Not sure why I'm avoiding you. Maybe I'm afraid that you aren't there. Certainly, I'm afraid of something. I still can't get myself to do much toning/sound or dance/movement when I'm alone. Why is that?

Dearest One,

We love you and want you to be happy and to know that you're the sweetest thing ever. We are fine with you just as you are. You have every right to choose not to sing and dance. If it's an obligation, we say don't do it, darling. If it scares you, that's because you're more powerful than you know. Power is one of those strange things that one wants but doesn't want. We say that you're doing fine as you write and eat and see clients and breathe and sleep. You don't have to do more than that.

We know you think that you should be growing in some extraordinary way. You write for gifted people, so you think you must get smarter and break through barriers to your higher consciousness. We say that you're perfect just as you are. No need for more growth. Do what draws you, not what scares you. Believe us. You're in the right place and the right time. It will become clear. Look at what you've done, dear, all on your own. You're a masterpiece. You can be safe. You can be quiet. You can take time to breathe and rest. What you are to do will become clear as you go. You are in a process. The writing is your thing right now, and it is glorious. In Japan. Italy. Brazil.

Holland. They love you all over. They wait to read your next words. THIS IS ENOUGH, dearest. More than enough.

You have found your voice, and it is powerful, beautiful, and spreading all over the world. Your intuition has taken you here. This is all your idea. It's all come from inside you. We so appreciate your kindness, your openness, your questing for perfection.

You're already perfect, dear one. We are here and always will be with you. Don't doubt that. We will not abandon you. We are here until the end and after the end. We thank you for doing this earthly rotation. We know it's a crazy assignment. You have great courage. We send you blessings and love. You're right on time, and all is well, quite well.

From "No Regrets"
(I wrote a version of the following for the website Highly Sensitive Refuge in 2022.)

On Being an Older RFM

I'm an Old(er) RFM.

I hate to admit it. I don't even believe it, but I'm seventy years old. I suspect seventy sounds old to you. It does to me. Medicare. Social Security. Bone scans. Lucky for me, in 2022, seventy is the new fifty, but still.

I can no longer say I'm middle-aged even though I feel about thirty-five. It's strange to be this old and to imagine the end is in sight. To be this age and think, *What do I have left to do? What do I want to be sure to say and do before it's too late? How have I lived? How have I loved? In what ways might I love more openly and deeply, and how might I continue to contribute to creating a more peaceful, sustainable world?*

Might I tell you about my life as an RFM to provide some guidance, reflection, and relief? Maybe even a little peace, harmony, and delight? Here's what I wish I had known when I was a youngster, like you, somewhere between zero and sixty-nine.

1. Sensitivity is cool. Being popular, loud, and boisterous is way overrated. I wish I had known I was not too sensitive, dramatic, moody, or annoying, but instead I was an RFM and had a rich, lush, complex personhood, which meant I had the right amounts of sensitivity, drama, moods, and annoyingness. It may be that popular, loud, and boisterous begets prom queens/kings. If you're no longer in high school, turn the pressure off. I remember thinking I was a wallflower and a wet blanket in those days. Now I hug that lonely teen and tell her, "Sensitivity is the real key to the kingdom."

2. Behind the scenes is where the power lies. It looks like the celebrities, the actors, and the famous athletes are having the most fun and wield the most influence. In reality, the writers, artists, stage managers, quirky quiet creators, and the tenderhearted are the ones to admire, the ones who change the world. Let's go change the world.

3. This one is embarrassing. I should have been less obsessed with my imperfect body and unruly hair. All the hours I spent straightening my hair I could have been learning Portuguese or signing up for a travel abroad program. When I thought I was not attractive enough, I could have realized that having smooth, nonsagging skin is beautiful, all you need, and should not be taken for granted.

4. Speaking of taking things for granted: breathing, walking, hearing, seeing, tasting, touching…you get the idea. I'm now not taking even the seemingly simple things for granted. You shouldn't either.

5. You're highly intuitive. It's part of the package. I would give myself more permission to explore the intuitive, the psychic, the metaphysical, and the spiritual much earlier. I might have found a sense of connection and belonging sooner. I did finally find it, and the connection has been so nourishing. We all need it for guidance, support, and love, especially during these times. Don't wait any longer.

6. I'm glad I had the good sense to get into psychotherapy in my thirties. I recommend it if you had any sort of dysfunctional family. Different types of therapies have made all the difference for me. I'm here writing to you today because of the healing I was able to do and continue to do. Inner work is often lifelong if you're deep, complex, and seeking to make a difference on planet earth, which many RFMs are determined to do.

7. About friends. Look for other RFMs when you are doing activities you enjoy. I've been good at this. I trust my intuition and find the people who are smart, bighearted, and sensitive, and I take the initiative to initiate and build the connection with them until they're able to reciprocate, realize how fortunate they are that I persisted, and see what an amazing friend I am! You can find good

friends at any age. It might be harder once you're out of school and living a busy life, but good friendships are essential. Make the time to find them, and feed those relationships. At the same time, some of your friendships may no longer be right for you. Allow them to fall away. There is only so much time in life; don't waste it with toxic friends. You'll need to learn how to say no more often. Chances are you have lots of compassion and want to help others, but yes is not always the right answer. It will be good to tune in to your deeper knowing and build healthy boundaries. I'm really good at saying no, and it has served me well.

8. About partners. This one has taken me the longest time to learn. I see the tendency in myself and my clients to choose partners who replicate patterns set up in childhood. It takes a lot of inner healing work to bring these patterns to consciousness and start to shift them, but if I can do it, so can you.

9. A combination of factors brings people together. It's a mystery, I suppose, but patterns from childhood are a big part of the mix. I knew this for years but still fell into the typical traps. In my case, I chose partners who were not willing to examine their childhood trauma and remained stuck in their depressive, anxious, limited states. They did not manage to grow along with me, and eventually the partnerships had to dissolve. I've come a long way healing from my past and letting go of ancestral legacies of suffering. I'm comfortable in my (sagging) skin and ready to receive and give some full-hearted, unambiguous love. This is a key to unlocking a healthy, thriving partnership. Take the time to get conscious of your unresolved issues if you're looking for love. If you're in a partnership, there are many resources for resolving conflicts and growing together. (At the moment, I'm single, so if my future partner is reading this, you know where to find me.)

10. About having children. I'm happily child-free. I always enjoyed being with kids and had an early career as a teacher, which I loved, but I was happy not to take them home with me. My introversion, sensitivity, and desire to create a fulfilling career combined to steer me away from a parenting lifestyle. I'm still content with that choice. Only a small twinge of doubt comes as I see my

friends with children and grandchildren, counting on their kids to be around if age-related disabilities rear their ugly heads. I would not want to burden my progeny with my ailments. There are better reasons to have children, and yet.

11. It may be a difficult choice for you, or you may have known all along that parenting was a deep desire or a clear no. Whether or not you choose the child-free road, self-care is a necessity. I'm your role model for that. You might say I'm the self-care queen, although I'm more the self-healing and preventive maintenance goddess. Over the years, I've been a client in therapy and explored many therapy modalities. I've seen other practitioners for acupuncture, energy work, massage, and more. This healing track also includes nutrition and other details that your sensitive body-mind needs for comprehensive care. Whether or not you have children, get on the self-care train.

12. Finally, trust yourself, and find your particular path or paths to your purpose. It's never too early or too late to imagine you're on earth for a reason and build the courage, strength, sense of humor, and self-confidence to access it. Be authentic. You don't need to follow anyone else's path even if it looks conventionally successful and everyone else seems to be doing it. You're already on the road, since you have identified as an RFM and are seeking more understanding.

What are your next steps? How are you living? How are you loving? In what ways might you love and be loved more openly and deeply, and how might you continue to contribute to creating a more peaceful sustainable life? So that, when you're seventy and speaking Portuguese, letting your hair go wild, and changing the world, you'll know exactly where your power lies.

Further Exploration

"

You have great compassion for others.
Let yourself receive some of that sweetness.
Forgive yourself for not being perfect.

Resources

Y ou may want to continue your inner work. In addition to the books mentioned, I recommend these books, workbooks, and Instagram sites.

These are not specific to rainforest minds but are excellent guides:

Doyle, G. (2020) *Untamed*. New York: Random House.

Doyle, G. *(2021) Get Untamed: The Journal*. New York: Random House.

Frost, S. (2010). *Soul Collage Evolving: An Intuitive Collage Process for Self-Discovery and Community*. CA: Hanford Mead.

Gottlieb, L. (2019) *Maybe You Should Talk to Someone: A Therapist, Her Therapist, and Our Lives Revealed*. New York: Houghton, Mifflin, Harcourt.

Gottlieb, L. (2021). *Maybe You Should Talk to Someone: The Workbook: A Toolkit for Editing Your Story and Changing Your Life*. WI: PESI.

Schwartz, R. (2021). *No Bad Parts: Healing Trauma & Restoring Wholeness with The Internal Family Systems Model*. CO: Sounds True.

Nedra Tawwab instagram.com/nedratawwab/

Yasmine Cheyenne instagram.com/yasminecheyenne/

Other important and related books:

Albere, P. (2017). *Evolutionary Relationships: Unleashing the Power of Mutual Awakening*. Virginia: Oracle Institute Press.

Baker, C., Harvey, A. (2022). *Radical Regeneration: Sacred Activism and the Renewal of the World.* Vermont: Inner Traditions.

Cain, S. (2022). *Bittersweet.* New York: Random House.

Maté, G. (2022). *The Myth of Normal: Trauma, Illness, & Healing in a Toxic Culture.* New York: Random House.

Ressa, M. (2022). *How to Stand Up to a Dictator: The Fight for Our Future.* New York: HarperCollins.

Solnit, R., Lutunatabua, T. eds. (2023). *Not Too Late: Changing the Climate Story from Despair to Possibility.* IL: Haymarket.

Resources on giftedness in adults:

Jacobsen, M. (1999). *The Gifted Adult.* New York: Ballantine.

Post, G. (2022). *The Gifted Parenting Journey.* Kentucky: Gifted Unlimited.

Prober, P. (2019) *Journey into Your Rainforest Mind: A Field Guide for Gifted Adults and Teens, Book Lovers, Overthinkers, Geeks, Sensitives, Brainiacs, Intuitives, Procrastinators, and Perfectionists.* Oregon: Luminare Press.

Prober, P. (2016) *Your Rainforest Mind: A Guide to the Well-Being of Gifted Adults and Youth.* Washington: GHF Press.

Instagram sites on journaling:

instagram.com/theisolationjournals/

instagram.com/soulfull.journaling/

instagram.com/journal.as.altar/

instagram.com/fiveminutejournal/

instagram.com/inspiringjournals/

Final Thoughts

want to thank my dearest clients, readers, friends, practitioners, and family for your feedback, encouragement, inspiration, suggestions, humor, listening, patience, guidance, hugs, insights, acceptance, sensitivity, and fan mail! And thank you, dear intrepid journaling explorers, for your courage and willingness to go on this introspective adventure with me. I feel so much gratitude for your oh so twisty turn-y, deep thought-y, and mystical realm-y BIG LOVE.

About the Author

I'm a psychotherapist, consultant, blogger, author, and tango dancer in private practice based in Eugene, Oregon. My clients over the past thirty-plus years have been intellectually and creatively gifted adults and parents of gifted children. Along with counseling in Oregon, I consult internationally. I have been a teacher of gifted children and presenter at universities, webinars, podcasts, and conferences. I have written articles on giftedness for *Psychotherapy Networker*, *Advanced Development Journal*, *The Register-Guard* and for online media such as *Thrive Global*, *Rebelle Society*, *Psychotherapy.net*, *Highly Sensitive Refuge*, and *Introvert Dear*.

I've written *Your Rainforest Mind: A Guide to the Well-Being of Gifted Adults and Youth*, an in-depth look at giftedness through case studies of my counseling clients; and *Journey into Your Rainforest Mind: A Field Guide for Gifted Adults and Teens, Book Lovers, Overthinkers, Geeks, Sensitives, Brainiacs, Intuitives, Procrastinators, and Perfectionists*, a collection of my most popular posts over the first four years of my blog (rainforestmind.com); and I can also be found creating memes and videos on Instagram. As of 2023, my newest project is an experiment in channeling sounds and songs for clients who then experience deep relaxation, personal insight, and a connection to their own spiritual guidance.

Made in the USA
Middletown, DE
06 February 2024

49216232R00139